THE DROOD MURDER CASE

THE DROOD MURDER CASE

Five Studies in
Dickens's Edwin Drood

RICHARD M. BAKER

Berkeley and Los Angeles 1951
UNIVERSITY OF CALIFORNIA PRESS

UNIVERSITY OF CALIFORNIA PRESS

BERKELEY AND LOS ANGELES

CALIFORNIA

◇

CAMBRIDGE UNIVERSITY PRESS

LONDON, ENGLAND

PRINTED IN THE UNITED STATES OF AMERICA
BY THE UNIVERSITY OF CALIFORNIA PRESS

TO MY SON

Richard Huddleston Baker

Introduction

ONE DAY about three years ago there came to my desk an article submitted for publication in *Nineteenth-Century Fiction* by Richard M. Baker, a scholar whom I did not then know. The object of his paper was to solve one of the many problems of Charles Dickens's uncompleted novel *The Mystery of Edwin Drood*. I had not at that time read very widely in the enormous bibliography of this subject, but what I had read had left me with the feeling that the various commentators were fumbling in the dark, guessing at hints of character development and plot motivation without textual substantiation. Mr. Baker's analysis, by contrast, seemed so knowing, so ingenious, and so convincing that I wrote him at once and expressed my hope that he would continue his illuminating studies. I then learned that Mr. Baker had devoted years to the study of *Edwin Drood* and that such a series of articles as I envisaged was already well advanced. The five studies which comprise the present volume were ultimately published in *Nineteenth-Century Fiction* in quarterly installments from March, 1948, through June, 1950. At the conclusion of the series Mr. Vincent Starrett, book columnist for the Chicago *Tribune* and editor of the best edition of *Edwin Drood,* called Mr. Baker's work "a knowledgeable, enthusiastic, and important contribution to a fascinating subject," and suggested that the five articles should be published in book form. We are very happy that it has been found possible to do this.

The Mystery of Edwin Drood is one of the most tantalizing of English novels. It is a superb murder mystery, first of all—highly dramatic and expertly written. The unfortunate fact of its incompleteness, Dickens having died mid-course, has perhaps heightened its interest. Ordinary readers have never tired of debating the issues. Several score of professional Dickensians have been driven to a close examination of the text and to a suggested solution of the unresolved action. A baker's dozen of "Droodians" (G. K. Chesterton called them "Druids") have actually completed the novel.

But there are two more points of interest: one concerns the development of Charles Dickens as a literary craftsman; the other concerns the development of Charles Dickens as a man. In construction *Edwin Drood* is notable among Dickens's novels. The usual mood of this writer was expansive. His exuberant fancy apparently could not find expression within a single plot. He rejected a simple melodic line for three-part or four-part harmonies. Subplots and supernumerary characters tumble prodigally through his exciting pages. The novel which immediately preceded *Edwin Drood* (1870) was *Our Mutual Friend* (1864–65). Never was there a more chaotic story: three main plots and a subplot for virtually every character. *Edwin Drood,* however, is tight, compact, highly unified. Every character, every action, is meaningful; there is not an irrelevant sentence. Between the two books Wilkie Collins had published *The Moonstone* (1868), one of the finest of all mystery novels. The friendship of Dickens and Collins had meanwhile ripened into an intimate companionship. Dickens admired the consummate craftsmanship of the less imaginative Collins, and there is no doubt that in *Edwin Drood* he put himself to the unaccustomed discipline of careful planning and set out to best Wilkie at his own game. The fragment that he left indicates that he was doing so by a very wide margin.

Edwin Drood was written in the bitterness of Dickens's deteriorating family life. He had separated from his wife in 1858, and because of the liaison with Ellen Ternan which followed in the

1860's he had suffered the estrangement of some of his children. That he was unhappy in these years there is no doubt. But that Charles Dickens and John Jasper, murderer of Edwin Drood, are one, which is Mr. Baker's brilliantly argued contention, has not, I believe, been previously suggested. In the story of another man who had killed the thing he loved Dickens was examining his own psychological processes, and, in a sense, expiating his own offense against society.

Though Dickens was well into the last third of his novel when he laid down his pen forever, it is significant of his skill as a master of suspense that no one of the crucial questions raised by the early chapters is answered. Was Edwin Drood murdered? Even this fundamental point is open to debate. Who was Dick Datchery, the white-thatched stranger who appears in Cloisterham to shadow John Jasper? Who was the Opium Woman, and what had she learned from her client's narcotic babbling that she set off at his heels? What use was to be made, plotwise, of the hints of Helena Landless's masculinity, of Mr. Bazzard's unexplained absence from Hiram Grewgious's chambers, of Edwin Drood's jewelery, of the special information of the crypt-master Durdles and his attendant imp Deputy?

It would be an unforgivable anticipation of Mr. Baker's discoveries for me to discuss his conclusions in any detail. But if I may judge from my own reaction to these studies, most readers will find the work of the literary detective almost as fascinating as the original narrative. With shrewd insight into the developing plot line and with amazing ingenuity in piecing together the broken hints of character revelation, Mr. Baker has reconstructed *The Mystery of Edwin Drood*. It may be pointed out that others have attempted this forbidding task with equal spirit, but that their arguments have not been able to withstand critical analysis. Without doubt Mr. Baker's thesis will be attacked by partisans of other solutions. Indeed, Mr. Edmund Wilson has already indicated at least a partial skepticism, though he has not yet made fully clear the grounds of his disagreement. I may say, however, that I have heard of no counterargument which Mr. Baker has not been able to demolish quickly and with finality.

Mr. Baker brings to his task valuable first-hand experience in the problems of the mystery novel. Professionally, he is Master of French at the Kent School, Kent, Connecticut. But for many years his avocation has been detective fiction. With the encouragement of S. S. Van Dine he wrote and published in 1936 his first mystery novel, *Death Stops the Manuscript.* This was followed in 1937 by *Death Stops the Rehearsal,* and in 1938 by *Death Stops the Bells.* Turning then to the study of Dickens, Mr. Baker devoted a number of years to a patient and meticulous study of *Edwin Drood.* The present volume is the culmination of this absorbing interest. At the moment he is engaged in an almost microscopic study of Dickens's original manuscript, hoping to wring from the emendations and cancellations further evidence to corroborate his deductions from the printed text. Meanwhile, I am happy to recommend his five studies to a wider audience than was perhaps reached through their journal publication.

BRADFORD A. BOOTH
Editor, *Nineteenth-Century Fiction*

Contents

Who Was Dick Datchery?

"MRS. TOPE's care has spread a very neat, clean breakfast ready for her lodger. Before sitting down to it, he opens his corner-cupboard door; takes his bit of chalk from its shelf; adds one thick line to the score, extending from the top of the cupboard door to the bottom; and then falls to with an appetite."

When Charles Dickens wrote these words in his little Swiss chalet on the eighth of June, 1870, he knew that he had come close to the end of the twenty-third chapter of *The Mystery of Edwin Drood*. He probably did not know that he was rapidly nearing the end of his life, or that what Shakespeare called the "fell sergeant" was to bring it to a close within a matter of hours. Chapter xxiii—as we have since learned—was underwritten by approximately two pages, and the novel itself was only half completed. Thus the untimely death of the second greatest creative genius in English literature left to posterity a mystery in a real sense; the fragment he had so aptly named was, furthermore, to break down into three additional mysteries, of which the first two have proved more compelling than the third. These further problems are best summed up by the questions they have posed. Was Edwin Drood actually murdered? Who was Dick Datchery? Who was the Opium Woman, and why did she pursue John Jasper so relentlessly? It is my present purpose to deal with the second of these questions.

Dick Datchery is first introduced to the reader at the very beginning of the eighteenth chapter. "At about this time a stranger appeared in Cloisterham; a white-haired personage, with black eyebrows. Being buttoned up in a tightish blue surtout, with a buff waistcoat and gray trousers, he had something of a military air; but he announced himself at the Crozier (the orthodox hotel, where he put up with a portmanteau) as an idle dog who lived upon his means; and he further announced that he had a mind to take a lodging in the picturesque old city for a month or two, with a view of settling down there altogether." In reality, he has come to the cathedral city to spy upon the activitiy of John Jasper and to learn all he can about him. Dickens describes him further. "This gentleman's white head was unusually large, and his shock of white hair was unusually thick and ample."

It has generally been asserted that Dick Datchery is an important character previously introduced in the novel who now comes to Cloisterham in disguise for the purpose of eventually clearing up the mystery of Edwin Drood's disappearance. Most of the writers who have dealt with Dickens's last work have had their say about the Datchery assumption—it was John Forster who first used this term—and have ingeniously proved him to be either Edwin Drood himself, or Neville Landless, or Helena Landless, or Lieutenant Tartar, or even the gloomy clerk Bazzard. Mr. Montagu Saunders, however, believes him to be an entirely new character, a man with a propensity for legal talk provided by the firm of solicitors to whom old Hiram Grewgious turned over his legal business. I shall endeavor to show that he was none of these, for the good and simple reason that he was, in my candid opinion, someone else.

I do, however, accept the general contention that Datchery is a personage already familiar to the reader but wearing a disguise, and before I attack the theories advanced by earlier Droodians to explain who he really is, I should like to discuss the disguise itself at some length. It consists chiefly of that shock of white hair which is so manifestly a wig, and an ample, uncomfortable one, at that. Datchery shakes it at the beginning of the chapter; later—in a passage which Dickens intended to cut from his manuscript when it was published, but which

Forster retained after Dickens was dead—he takes off his hat to give it another shake. Before the eighteenth chapter comes to an end, we have no fewer than three references to Datchery walking along with his hat under his arm and his white hair streaming in the breeze. Perhaps because he was aware that he had reiterated this fact once too often, Dickens deleted the second reference; but again, Forster left it in when the sixth monthly installment of the story was printed. In the twenty-third chapter, where Datchery makes his second appearance, the white hair has become gray—a minor slip of which even the great writers are capable—but the large head (or wig) is there, and once more its owner lounges along "with his uncovered gray hair blowing about."

Now it seems to me fairly evident that Datchery wants people to see him without his hat; that he deliberately invites their scrutiny of his white mane. And here we should remember the black eyebrows, which not only form a striking contrast to the white hair, but serve to arouse an inclination on the part of a person beholding Datchery to contemplate the upper part of his face. Dickens, an amateur actor of unusual talent, who first grew his full beard to play more realistically a part in Wilkie Collins's drama *The Frozen Deep*, was too well acquainted with make-up to indulge in false whiskers and grease paint; he relies upon the disparity in color between Datchery's hair and eyebrows to alter the appearance of a person who would otherwise be recognized by several of the inhabitants of Cloisterham. That Datchery's eyebrows have been dyed black to conceal their natural color is a foregone conclusion. That the wig has been selected for a similar reason is likewise evident, although the choice of contrasting color is deliberate. For all we know to the contrary, Datchery may have reminded this or that dweller in Cloisterham who came in contact with him of the individual whom I believe him to be; Dickens does not tell us so, of course, for it would have defeated his purpose.

The true identity of Datchery was to have been one of the major points of interest in the story; witness the fact that so many writers have been concerned with the assumption. And I

shall endeavor to show that Dickens played fair with the reader
by giving many a subtle hint of who Datchery really is. I am
not at all convinced that Dickens had the assumption in mind
when he wrote as follows to John Forster on Friday, August 6,
1869: "I laid aside the fancy I told you of, and have a very
curious and new idea for my new story. Not a communicable
idea (or the interest of the book would be gone), but a very
strong one, though difficult to work." Nevertheless, I do feel
certain that he was thinking of the Datchery assumption when
he penned the following letter to James T. Fields:

> 5 Hyde Park Place, London, W.
> Friday, Fourteenth January 1870
>
> Forster (who has been ill with his bronchitis again) thinks No. 2 of the
> new book (Edwin Drood) a clincher,—I mean that word (as his own
> expression) for *Clincher*. There is a curious interest steadily working
> up to No. 5, which requires a great deal of art and self-denial. I think
> also, apart from character and picturesqueness, that the young couple
> are placed in a very novel situation. So I hope—at Nos. 5 and 6 the
> story will turn upon an interest suspended until the end.

I do not need to inform any reader familiar with the story
that Datchery makes his only appearances in the fifth and sixth
monthly parts, to which Dickens refers in his last sentence, and
it seems clear to me that the "interest suspended until the end"
refers to the Datchery assumption. Indeed, Forster tells us that
Dickens was worried because it was introduced too early in
Part V; it seems as if he were afraid that some clever readers
might penetrate the disguise and perceive the true identity of
the white-haired stranger. Forster, as editor of the story after
Dickens's death, is responsible for the position of chapter xviii
as it now appears in the printed version. In the manuscript, it
was originally chapter xix, and Professor Jackson has demonstrated with considerable logic that it might well have been
placed between the present chapters xxii and xxiii. Who, then,
was Dick Datchery, who was to have so important a part in the
subsequent development of the plot, and whose efforts were
ultimately to fasten the guilt for the murder of Edwin Drood
upon that unhappy young man's uncle, John Jasper?

As I consider the theories of earlier writers only to disagree with their conclusions; as I develop my own conception of who Datchery really is, I shall try to be mindful of the words of J. Cuming Walters, who gave so much thought to the mystery, and who wrote so prolifically about it. He said—and this might well be a maxim for many a commentator,—"No conclusion can be held to be good and justified which departs from Dickens's own lines." A little later on in the same volume, Mr. Walters likewise echoes the old query: "Who was Datchery? This is the actual mystery. This was the surprise Dickens had in store, steadily working up from the first. And it says much for his triumph that either this point has been belittled or entirely overlooked." It would seem that Mr. Walters also had read the letter which Dickens wrote to James T. Fields.

Messrs. Proctor, Lang, Archer, and Carr are of the opinion that Edwin Drood himself was Dick Datchery. They believe that the young man somehow escaped from the encircling folds of Jasper's great black scarf, death by strangulation, and the corrosive quicklime into which the uncle planned to throw his nephew's body. They overlook the weight of the evidence contained in Forster's remarks concerning the general content of the novel as Dickens himself had outlined it to him—remarks which follow immediately after his quotation from the author's letter of Friday, August 6, 1869. They do not take into account the statement made by Sir Luke Fildes, the famous illustrator of *Edwin Drood*, in his splendid letter to the Editor of *The Times*. They pass lightly over the testimony of Charles Dickens the younger and of Madame Perugini, the novelist's daughter. All this valuable material has been presented in earlier studies; to introduce it here in detail would be mere repetition, but it leaves me convinced that Edwin Drood was murdered.

Perhaps the circumstances resulting in a letter written by Charles Dickens to the Hon. Robert Lytton might be cited as additional proof that Edwin Drood actually met death at the hands of his uncle. The Hon. Robert Lytton had written a story entitled *John Acland*, the plot of which was remarkably similar to that of *Edwin Drood*, begun at a later date. Lytton's story concerned the murder of a man by his closest friend; the body could not be discovered, yet there was the intimation that the murdered man might still be alive. At last the *corpus delicti* was found in an icehouse, and its identity was proved by means of a watch. Publication of this story, which was begun in *All the Year Round*, the magazine of which Dickens was editor, was abruptly terminated because he declared that the plot had been used before. Despite this fact, he was himself to make use of a similar idea some six months later. Prior to the suspension of the tale, however, he had written to the Hon. Robert Lytton as follows:

26, Wellington Street, London
Thursday, Second September, 1869

My dear Robert Lytton,—John Acland is most willingly accepted, and shall come into the next monthly part. I shall make bold to condense him here and there (according to my best idea of story-telling), and particularly where he makes the speech:—And with the usual fault of being too long, here and there, I think you let the story out too much—prematurely—and this I hope to prevent artfully. I think your title open to the same objection, and therefore propose to substitute:

The Disappearance
of John Acland.

This will leave the reader in doubt whether he really *was* murdered, until the end.

When one considers the striking similarity existing between the plots of *John Acland* and *Edwin Drood*, and when one turns to the few original notes which Dickens left behind him at his death and which had served to guide him in the writing of his own novel, one is surprised to find that among several tentative titles listed by the novelist is "The Disappearance of Edwin Drood," followed immediately by the title which the story bears today. If, in the mind of Dickens, "The Disappearance of John Acland" would leave the reader in doubt whether a man were really murdered or not, why would not the word "mystery" answer a similar purpose? This conclusion is strengthened by the fact that two other titles under consideration were "James's Disappearance" and "The Mystery in the Drood Family."

No, Edwin Drood was really dead, and "the very curious and new idea" of which Dickens spoke to Forster was not Edwin's return to Cloisterham in the guise of Datchery for the purpose of confounding his wicked uncle. Strangely enough, Edwin is never described to any extent by Dickens; the most we know about his external appearance is gleaned from a greeting given him by the matronly Tisher when he comes to visit Rosa at the Nuns' House. "I hope I see Mr. Drood well," she says, "though I needn't ask, if I may judge from his complexion." From that remark, one might deduce ruddy cheeks; but we are never told the color of Edwin's eyes or of his hair. It would almost seem as if Dickens neglected to portray Edwin's outward appearance because he knew that the young man was to disappear from the scene forever. We do learn later, however, in the course of this same visit, that Edwin has had half his hair cut off. I suspect that Rosa's statement to this effect has been introduced by Dickens as a red herring; he may have felt that some readers would associate Edwin's cropped poll with the wig worn by Datchery. But there is no further reference to the shorn locks, so the red herring may be consigned to the dustbin.

There is really very little about Edwin to endear him to us, or to cause us any degree of anguish when he disappears. Indeed, he is sometimes too smug and self-satisfied to invite affection. He has drifted away from Rosa and has become interested in Helena Landless. In this "off with the old love, on with the new" mood, somewhat dampened by his conversation with the Opium Woman, he goes to the supper party on that stormy Christmas Eve and is done to death by his uncle. He is a youth of honor nonetheless, and I doubt that, had he been alive, he would ever have remained in concealment while Neville Land-less brooded under a cloud of suspicion as his murderer. He had promised Grewgious to return the ring of diamonds and rubies which had belonged to Rosa's mother, should circumstances make it impossible for him to place it upon the finger of the young woman pledged from childhood to be his fiancée; he would undoubtedly have kept his promise had he been in a position to do so after he and Rosa broke their engagement and

parted as brother and sister. From an artistic point of view as
well as from the exigencies of the plot Edwin must be dead.
There will be no Rosa to whom he might return, for she has become enamored of the agile Lieutenant Tartar; and Helena
Landless, of whom he had begun to dream, will eventually become the wife of Minor Canon Crisparkle. Dickens had often
used the "watched by the dead" idea, but he was not to do so
again in his last novel. Edwin Drood, undoubtedly his uncle's
victim, is not Dick Datchery.

What of Neville Landless, favored by Messrs. Stephens and
Lang, as the stranger who appeared in Cloisterham? Dickens
himself rules out this possibility when he first describes young
Landless. Since this description involves both Neville and his
twin sister Helena, so that the two are inextricably intermin-
gled, I shall quote the passage referring to them in full, and then
return to it later when I speak of Miss Landless as a contestant
for the role of Datchery. "An unusually handsome lithe young
fellow, and an unusually handsome lithe girl; much alike; both
very dark, and very rich in colour; she of almost the gipsy type;
something untamed about them both; a certain air upon them of
hunter and huntress; yet withal a certain air of being the objects
of the chase, rather than the followers." Objects of the chase,
rather than the followers. But Datchery is a follower, spying
upon Jasper, learning all he can about him, waiting until the
time shall be propitious to prove him the murderer of his
nephew. Neville Landless is temperamental, proud, and impetuous; he is the ideal type of man upon whom to fasten blame
for a murder, as Jasper quickly perceives. But Dickens goes out
of his way to show us that Neville is guiltless of Edwin's death:
the preparations for his walking tour are logically made, so that
he may not be a source of embarrassment to anyone after his
unfortunate quarrel with Edwin, cleverly fomented by Jasper.
But above all, he wants to be away from Rosa, whom he has
come to love at first sight with a love which he has given his
sacred pledge to keep hidden from the object of his passion.
When he reappears after the tempestuous Christmas Eve upon
which Edwin met his death, we find him sitting in the sanded

parlor of the Tilted Wagon, a roadside tavern eight miles distant from Cloisterham. And what are his thoughts? He is "wondering in how long a time after he had gone, the sneezy fire of damp fagots would begin to make somebody else warm." Certainly this is not the conjecture of a murderer, unless he be made of vastly different stuff.

Besides, when he is in London a good six months after having been apprehended and brought before the authorities, detained and redetained, and finally released because the body of Edwin Drood is still missing, he is even then so much oppressed by the shadow of suspicion hanging over him that he cannot go out into the streets—even at night—without feeling marked and tainted. Only the friendly visits and constant encouragement of Minor Canon Crisparkle, who has induced him to study for the law, together with the example of fortitude set him by his sister's conduct, enable him to struggle on in the hope that time and circumstances may vindicate his name. A man living day by day in this sort of mental and physical seclusion, a man who looks upon himself as a social pariah, could not suddenly appear in Cloisterham in the guise of Dick Datchery, jovial, urbane, a shrewd judge of human nature and gifted with legal ability to ask leading questions in a subtle way which masks their true purpose. Again I suspect a red herring when Neville says to Crisparkle: "Excellent circumstances for study, anyhow! and you know, Mr. Crisparkle, what need I have of study in all ways. Not to mention that you have advised me to study for the difficult profession of the law, specially, and that of course I am guiding myself by the advice of such a friend and helper." Neville is but a novice in this difficult profession, whereas Datchery is an old, experienced hand. By no possible exercise of the imagination can I conceive of Neville Landless as Dick Datchery.

It was Mr. J. Cuming Walters who evolved the startling theory that Neville's sister Helena was Dick Datchery. His ideas on the subject are succinctly expressed in his thoroughly interesting book, *The Complete Mystery of Edwin Drood*. As recently as 1939, in a lecture to the students of English 354 given

during the summer at the University of Chicago, Mr. Edmund
Wilson stated that this solution was the "first of the important
discoveries about *Drood*." Despite the brilliance of Mr. Walters's
argument and the opinion expressed by Mr. Wilson, I am forced
to disagree with both gentlemen. In order to disprove the theory
advanced by Mr. Walters, I shall have to summarize his con-
tentions and quote him at some length.

After stating that the problem of Edwin Drood has been set
forth in the first sixteen chapters of the novel, Mr. Walters remarks that all the important characters have already been introduced: it would be the "worst of tricks" if an indispensable fact
or person were to be brought in later. He then rules out Lieutenant Tartar and Bazzard—with whom I shall deal later—as
possibilities for the role of Datchery. Finally he asserts that
Helena Landless is "revealed from the first and fully developed"
for the Datchery assumption.

"Who would be selected?" he goes on to ask. "Obviously a
courageous, and, if possible, an experienced person; a person
with a real interest, and with a decided incentive; a person with
suspicion already excited; a person impelled to activity not only
by what had already happened but by what was likely to
happen." A little later on he adds: "The stimulus must come
from within; there must be a reason in the heart itself."

These are excellent sentiments, with which I agree most
heartily, but they do not characterize Helena Landless with
half the emphasis they gain when used to qualify another personage. And the same is true of Mr. Walters's additional remark:
"We must look to the beginning of the story for this essential
person. And that person must have motive and capacity."

What, according to Mr. Walters, is Helena's motive for dis-
guising herself as Datchery? She has, he tells us, an instinctive
hatred, but no fear, of Jasper; and she has the threefold desire
not only to avenge Edwin Drood, but also to save her brother
and to save Rosa. I have no objection to the second part of this
motive; it is undoubtedly true that Helena would be ready to
do anything within reason to clear her brother of the cloud of
suspicion hanging over him. But whatever she might have done

in that part of the novel which Dickens carried with him to the grave, she would have done under the guidance of Minor Canon Crisparkle, for whom she has a deep admiration bordering on love, and under the direction of Hiram Grewgious. She had a peculiar, telepathic ability to see through Jasper and to read his mind; she was almost instantly aware of his passion for Rosa—a passion little short of lust—and it was naturally revolting to her. A far stronger character than her brother, she was prompt to spring to the defense of a woman younger than herself, especially a woman of so childlike a nature as Rosa, and in that respect she did have a motive for protecting her friend from Jasper's unwelcome attentions. But I have been unable to discover that she had any incentive to avenge the death of Edwin. She knew that her brother was in love with Rosa, and I suggest that it would have been only a natural, human instinct on her part to hope that some day, when his name had been cleared of suspicion, Neville might honorably avow his love to Rosa and propose marriage. When she first realizes that Rosa has become interested in Lieutenant Tartar, Helena's immediate reaction is compassionate concern for Neville.

"She was experienced," says Mr. Walters. "As a child she had dressed as a boy and shown the daring of a man—why should we be told this so precisely if she were not to play a masculine part again?" Why indeed? Mr. Walters might have added that, upon the occasion to which he refers, Helena tried to tear out, or bite off, her hair when Neville lost the pocket knife with which she was to have cut it short. Of course, Dickens had a motive in giving the reader this aspect of Helena the untamed. Some day I hope to show that she was to play the part of a man—but not that of Datchery. It is far more likely that she was to confront Jasper in the likeness of her twin brother, dressed in his clothes, in a scene of great import. Does not Dickens tell us that Helena and Neville were "much alike; both very dark, and very rich in colour"? How could Dickens have played fair with the reader when he described the white hair and black eyebrows of Datchery, if he had left out this richness of color? No, the reference to Helena's assuming the disguise of a man on several occasions is just another red herring so far as Dick Datchery is concerned.

"At an early stage we are told of her threat against Jasper," Mr. Walters continues. "Why should she threaten if she was to do nothing? When Rosa was frightened at Jasper, Helena's dark eyes 'gleamed with fire,' and the warning was uttered—'Let whomsoever is most concerned look well to it.' Jasper was the person concerned—was the warning meaningless?"

By no means. But again, Helena was eventually to come to grips with Jasper in the guise of her brother Neville, not in the person of Dick Datchery, the idle buffer living on his means.

And now Mr. Walters becomes even more precise: "The big wig, unnecessary in a man, is essential to a woman with profuse locks. The surtout, unnecessary in a man (and worn, by the way, in fine weather), was essential to conceal the woman's figure. A man does not forget his hat, even when wearing a wig, but a woman with a wig on her own luxuriant hair would be liable to do so. Datchery 'shook his hair.' Men do *not* shake their hair. Datchery 'made a leg'—practically the curtsey of a woman. Datchery let his hair 'stream in the wind.' Only a woman would have been unembarrassed by that."

I have not been able to find, at any point in his descriptions of Datchery, that Dickens uses the adjective "big" with reference to Datchery's crop of hair, although I believe it to be a wig and not a natural growth. He does employ the term "shock of white hair" several times, and states that Datchery's head was unusually large. For a successful disguise the wig must have fitted snugly; otherwise it might have come off at a crucial moment. If a man's head is large, the wig he wears will have to be correspondingly large. If the hair of such a wig is unusually thick and ample, we shall probably speak of the ensemble as a "large," even a "big" wig; but it does not necessarily follow that it has to be of this size to go over a woman's profuse locks. And by the same token, the long hair of such a wig will naturally "stream in the wind" if the wind is blowing.

As to the surtout, it is described by Dickens as "tightish." This being so, would it not bring some discomfort to Helena's bosom, and reveal rather than conceal it? Since she was almost of the gypsy type, I can hardly picture her as a flat-chested female. And if the person disguised as Datchery were elderly, I can conceive of the surtout being worn even in fine weather. An elderly person—especially a man of advanced years—requires warmer covering than a young, warm-blooded woman.

Datchery does not actually forget his hat, as Mr. Walters seems to imply, for Dickens himself says: "All this time Mr. Datchery had walked with his hat under his arm, and his white hair streaming. He had an odd momentary appearance upon him of having forgotten his hat, when Mr. Sapsea now touched it; and he clapped his hand up to his head as if with some vague expectation of finding another hat upon it." The "appearance" of having forgotten the hat is precisely stated as a "momentary" one, it should be noted, and Datchery could not have been un- aware for any length of time that he had it under his arm. The purpose of this passage, as I see it, is to inform the reader—not bluntly, but in a roundabout fashion—that Datchery is wearing a wig. Now the wig may well have felt like a hat, which would account for Datchery's gesture. Dickens certainly conveys the idea that Datchery was conscious of *something* resting on his head, and in phraseology typically Dickensian invites the reader to wonder what it might be.

"Men do *not* shake their hair," affirms Mr. Walters. I concede that this is not an ordinary procedure on the part of members of the male sex; but what if a habitual, revealing action closely connected with the head is denied a man if he is playing the part of another person, and wearing an uncomfortable wig to boot? Such a habitual action, in this particular instance, might displace the wig, so what could the wearer thereof do but shake the hair?

Datchery "made a leg," to be sure, but it was in the presence of that pompous ass, Mayor Sapsea, and was done for a definite purpose. Datchery was playing up to the mayor's inflated ego- tism in every way; to bow the knee, as it were, was a clever form of flattery, a sop to Sapsea's exalted idea of his own importance; it does not indicate a woman.

Mr. Walters glosses over Datchery's meal of "fried sole, veal cutlet and a pint of sherry" by saying that Helena was robust, and that since she was acting the part of a man she would naturally call for a man's meal. I have no fault to find with this argument; I shall simply state that the meal is also typical of the person whom I have in mind as Datchery, and that his predilection for fine wines is established by the author early in the story. Mr. Walters is absolutely right when he concludes that the meal "is absolutely non-committal."

"It has been objected," continues Mr. Walters, "that Helena would not use chalk-marks as a score. Why not? Any woman can use a piece of chalk; the old tavern custom is well-known; and it would appeal to a person who did not wish to be betrayed by handwriting. It is exactly the sort of device a woman would adopt. Of course, there was no need to keep a score at all—it was merely byplay, and very feminine byplay, too."

I do not disagree with the first part of Mr. Walters's last sentence; but I mean to prove that the keeping of the score was one of the most characteristic traits of the man who is really Datchery.

"It is contended that Datchery's conversation is not like Helena's. That is no argument, because it is not like anybody's in the story. It was an obvious artifice. But now we have to think of capacity. Datchery's sentences are long, flowing, and easy. Helena's conversation was fluent, even eloquent."

Here Mr. Walters lays himself open to contradiction. Datchery's conversation is very like that of someone else in the story, as I shall show presently. And some of his sentences—later to be reproduced—are short almost to the point of curtness. Indeed, Datchery alternates between curtness and fluency, and he uses expressions of which Helena would never have been capable. I simply cannot imagine Helena—for all the capacity Mr. Walters might give her—uttering the following words: "Even a diplomatic bird must fall to such a gun."

"Datchery spoke 'in a low tone,'" says Mr. Walters, quoting briefly—and incorrectly—from the text. "Helena, we are told, had 'a low, rich voice'—just suitable for Datchery." But upon what occasion did he speak in this way, and under what circumstances? It was when the Opium Woman came upon him sitting in the vaulted room he had rented from Mrs. Tope, and when Jasper, pursued by the crone, had just gone up the stairs. Let us examine the complete text. "Halloa!" he cries in a low voice, seeing her brought to a standstill: "who are you looking for?" Notice the verb: Datchery "cries" in a low voice. He is naturally startled by this apparition, this ugly hag who interrupts his writing, so he cries out. But Dickens makes him do so in a low voice because Datchery knows that Jasper has ascended the stairs only a moment before; he may not yet have entered his room and closed the door; he may even be eavesdropping. Surprise tempered by caution is all I can read from this passage; it scarcely proves that Datchery spoke habitually in low tones.

"Helena's movements are compatible with her acting the part of Datchery. She disappears—and, strangely enough, we are not told where. She reappears in London just at the moment she could be spared from Cloisterham. Datchery is then heard of again in Cloisterham, and this time Helena is not to be traced. An amazing conjunction of circumstances—as Helena goes, Datchery comes. Was it accidental?"

I do not fully understand what Mr. Walters means by saying: "She disappears—and, strangely enough, we are not told where." When Minor Canon Crisparkle visits Neville in his gloomy room at Staple Inn six months after Edwin's disappearance, he says to the youth: "Next week, you will cease to be alone, and will have a devoted companion." "And yet this seems an uncongenial place to bring my sister to," Neville replies. It would appear that Helena is still at Miss Twinkleton's school, waiting for the end of term. The conversation I have cited occurs in chapter xvii of the novel, and we know as a result of the brilliant work done by Professor Jackson that the events of chapter xviii, which follows immediately in the ordinary version and in which Datchery first appears, were prematurely introduced in the chronological pattern of the novel. Now in the very first paragraph of chapter xix—which should have been chapter xviii— we are told: "Once again Miss Twinkleton has delivered her vale-

dictory address, with the accompaniments of white-wine and
pound-cake, and again the young ladies have departed to their
several homes. Helena Landless has left the Nuns' House to
attend her brother's fortunes, and pretty Rosa is alone." Then
comes the ugly scene in the garden by the sun dial; we may be
sure that Jasper hastened to Rosa as soon as he possibly could
after the close of school. As a result of her ordeal with Jasper,
Rosa flees to her guardian, Grewgious, in London—and there,
on the very day after her arrival, she meets Helena, who has
obviously come to look after her brother, precisely as Dickens
has told us. I do not see how this natural visit can be termed a
"disappearance." As for the final chapter of the novel, it is devoted primarily to Jasper, to the Opium Woman, and to Datchery.
It is true that it contains no reference to Helena's whereabouts—already well enough established,—but it seems far-
fetched to conclude, just because of this fact, that she is not to
be traced. Presumably she is still in London, caring for her
brother.

No, despite the ingenuity displayed by Mr. Walters, he does
not persuade me that Helena Landless is Dick Datchery. And it
should be remembered that in *The Mystery of Edwin Drood*,
Dickens was admittedly attempting to outdo his friend, Wilkie
Collins; the younger author had achieved great success with
The Moonstone, considered by some critics to have the most perfect plot of any story of the type ever written. Dickens, who
published it, had not approved of the method by means of which
Collins unfolded the history of the yellow diamond, but he did
recognize the general excellence of the narrative, and it was a
challenge to him to create something in a similar vein. Now the
idea of a young girl assuming male disguise had already been
developed by Collins in *No Name*. It is hardly conceivable that
Dickens, deliberately setting out to surpass him at his own
game, would have employed the same device in one of the major
aspects of *Edwin Drood*.[1] If Helena is to masquerade as a man,
she will impersonate her twin brother, as I have already sug-

[1] Long after I had arrived at this conclusion, I was fortunate enough to purchase a
copy of R. C. Lehmann's *Charles Dickens as Editor*. This book contains a large collection

gested, and so make good the warning directed against Jasper; she will not turn out to be the chief detecting personality at the very center of the interest which Dickens planned to keep suspended from Parts V and VI of the novel up to the end.

I turn now to Lieutenant Tartar, created to supplant the memory of Edwin in Rosa's mind and affections and undoubtedly designed to play an important part in the final tracking down of Jasper. Messrs. Smetham, Gadd, and Carden have reached the conclusion that he is Dick Datchery. Here again, I contend that Dickens has made it utterly impossible to consider this energetic young man for the role of Datchery by the rather detailed description he gives of him. We first meet Tartar in chapter xvii, when he is discovered by Neville in the latter's rooms. Dickens depicts him thus: "A handsome young gentleman, with a young face, but with an older figure in its robustness and its breadth of shoulder; say a man of eight-and-twenty, or at the utmost thirty; so extremely sun-burnt that the contrast between his brown visage and the white forehead shaded out of doors by his hat, and the glimpses of white throat below the neckerchief, would have been almost ludicrous but for his broad temples, bright blue eyes, clustering brown hair, and laughing teeth." I suggest that Tartar's white forehead would have been equally as ludicrous had he worn Datchery's wig and dyed his eyebrows black. Indeed, his eyebrows, so darkened, would have attracted even greater attention to his pale forehead and brown face. It will be recalled that Datchery went about hatless most of the time, with the deliberate purpose, as I believe, of inviting attention to the marked contrast between his white hair and

---

of letters written by the novelist to W. H. Wills through the years when the latter was subeditor of *Household Words* and *All the Year Round*. In one of these letters, Dickens refers to *The Moonstone* as follows:

Gad's Hill Place
Higham by Rochester, Kent,
Sunday, Thirtieth June, 1867

My Dear Wills:—I have heard read the first 3 Nos. of Wilkie's story this morning, and have gone minutely through the plot of the rest to the last line. Of course it is a series of "Narratives," and of course such and so many modes of action are open to such and such people; but it is a very curious story—wild, and yet domestic—with excellent character in it, great mystery, and *nothing belonging to disguised women or the like*. [The italics are mine.]

The words I have put in italics appear to confirm the conclusion I had already formed prior to my discovery of this letter.

black eyebrows. Tartar, on the other hand, must have worn his hat habitually when out of doors, to achieve the disparity in color emphasized by Dickens.

In his conversation with Neville at their first meeting, Tartar remarks at one point: "I am always afraid of inconveniencing busy men, being an idle man." Some writers have straightway pounced upon the adjective "idle" to link it with Datchery's characterization of himself as "an idle buffer." Here, they exclaim, is the proof that Tartar and Datchery are one and the same person. Now it may well be that Dickens employed the qualification in this instance as a minor red herring; it is likewise evident that the word "idle" is a very common opposite of the adjective "busy."

Lieutenant Tartar, who is extremely polite and apologetic, is fond of neatness and orderliness in everything; Dickens dwells at length upon the impeccable, shipshape appearance of his rooms. Datchery, on the contrary, when he seeks lodgings in Cloisterham, calls for something odd and out of the way, venerable, architectural, and inconvenient. Assuming for the moment that Tartar did adopt the disguise of Datchery, I maintain that he would not so far have violated the fastidious side of his nature as to demand rooms of such a type, even though he were bent on playing the part of the white-haired stranger right up to the hilt. Such fidelity to his conception of a person he was enacting would have been quite unnecessary, if not psychologically impossible. Furthermore, since he was unknown to any of the inhabitants of the cathedral city, there would have been no incentive for him to put on any disguise whatsoever.

It is interesting to note that Tartar smokes, whereas Datchery does not. Now a man addicted to smoking would find it extremely difficult to forego that pleasure if he were playing the part of another, especially when there would not be the slightest reason to refrain from indulging in the habit.

In point of fact, Tartar does not know anything about the crisis which so much occupies the thoughts and emotions of those most deeply concerned in it when he first meets them. He is willing to be of service, and declares his readiness to see Neville openly and often—indeed, almost daily. He has made this promise indirectly to Helena, fully aware that Miss Landless is devoted to Rosa and that she has a great deal of influence over the lovely young creature who has already made an impression upon him. We may be sure that he will keep this promise—perhaps a little more literally than Rosa would have desired, as is evidenced by her anxiety when the gritty state of affairs comes on, when day after day goes by without the slightest sign from the handsome lieutenant. Yes, Tartar is extremely forthright; he will make it a point to frequent Neville.

I do not believe that Tartar, late of the Royal Navy, would have made any comment—or certainly not the one that is made—on the term employed by Deputy when that impish boy was being questioned about the Opium Woman. The episode to which I refer occurs in the twenty-third chapter. Datchery, intensely interested in the crone because of revelations she has made concerning Edwin, encounters Deputy and plies him with questions. At one point of the interrogation, we have the following dialogue, begun by Datchery.

"What is her name?"

"'Er Royal Highness the Princess Puffer."

"She has some other name than that; where does she live?"

"Up in London. Among the Jacks."

"The sailors?"

Tartar, had he been Datchery, would never have made that query; he would have recognized the term immediately as the abbreviation of the colloquial expression "jack-tar," having been a sailor himself.

Tartar is too young and inexperienced a person to have assumed the role of Datchery, and he is totally lacking in the knowledge of things legal evinced by the white-haired stranger. His failure to call upon Rosa during the days following their idyllic trip on the river, so eagerly seized upon by those who assert that he is the man of mystery who appeared in Cloisterham, is just another of the many red herrings which Dickens has drawn across the trail leading to the final solution of the problem.

Bazzard, "a gloomy person with tangled locks," who fulfilled in a highly ambiguous manner the duties of clerk to Grewgious, may likewise be removed from the list of contestants for the role of Dick Datchery. How does Dickens describe him, when we first make his acquaintance? "A pale, puffy-faced, dark-haired person of thirty, with big dark eyes that wholly wanted lustre, and a dissatisfied doughy complexion, that seemed to ask to be sent to the baker's, this attendant was a mysterious being, possessed of some strange power over Mr. Grewgious."

I find it hard to believe that writers like Messrs. Charles, Matchett, Odgers, Fitzgerald, Macdermott, and R. H. Newell, whose pseudonym was Orpheus C. Kerr, should select this minor character as the man who was Dick Datchery. When Bazzard speaks—he does so but rarely,—it is with a brevity bordering upon rudeness. He is vain, surly, and moody; his nature and Datchery's are antipodal. He is one of those innumerable characters, sharply and deftly drawn, whom Dickens created to play subordinate, albeit important, parts. I can think of only one reason why Bazzard should be at all essential to the plot of the novel so far as it is developed in the fragment which remains to us. I can think of only one reason why he should be essential to the concluding chapters of the story which Dickens carried with him to the grave. He was a witness to the fact that the ring of diamonds and rubies passed literally from the keeping of Grewgious into that of Edwin; he was present—although just roused from deep slumber caused by rich food and drink—when the lawyer handed the case containing the jeweled band to young Drood.

Much has been made of the information given Rosa by Grewgious when he said, with reference to Bazzard: "In fact, he is off duty here, altogether, just at present." The gloomy clerk's adherents say there is proof positive that he was even then walking the streets of Cloisterham in the guise of Datchery. They cast aside the evidence indicating that Dickens intended to place the white-haired stranger's advent in Cloisterham at a date much later than that upon which Grewgious made his statement. I have no doubt that Dickens intended them to react in this very manner. But Grewgious had sent Bazzard away for quite a different reason—a reason which was soon to be revealed, and which I feel certain was in some subsidiary way connected with "The Thorn of Anxiety," that famous tragedy written by Bazzard, with a title typical of the man himself, but never produced.

It has been suggested that Bazzard may have become a tool of John Jasper, and that he may have told Jasper about the ring which Edwin still carried with him, all unbeknown to his uncle, the night he was murdered. Only three persons knew about the gold band set with jewels, to which Dickens gave such significance: Grewgious, Edwin Drood, and Bazzard. But had Grewgious entertained the slightest suspicion that his clerk would ally himself in any way with Jasper, he would never have lodged Rosa, whom he had sworn to protect from Jasper's machinations, in the home of Mrs. Billickin, a widowed cousin of Bazzard's, "divers times removed." The shrewd old lawyer would certainly have foreseen the possibility that Bazzard might learn of Rosa's presence in his cousin's home, and had he doubted his clerk's integrity he would never have placed his ward in a position of such potential danger.

Had Bazzard been Datchery, he would have had no need of wearing a disguise in Cloisterham. He, too, was completely unknown to the inhabitants. Furthermore, there is no reason to suppose that a writer of tragedies—presumably mediocre—is also an actor, and Bazzard would have had to be a very great actor indeed to have played the part of Datchery as we know him. Even if he had been eager to attempt a role of such difficulty, Grewgious would never have entrusted so delicate a mission, in so vital a situation, to so lumpish a man.

Who, then, was Dick Datchery?

J. Cuming Walters, despite his theory that Helena Landless was Datchery, for which I have taken him to task at some length, came far nearer than he realized to the heart of the matter and to a logical solution of the oft-reiterated question. In his short but provocative book, *Clues to Dickens's "Mystery of Edwin Drood,"* he said: "Part of a further surprise in the story would have awaited the reader in finding that in this tale,

without an orthodox hero and with but a very uncertain heroine, the real hero and heroine in moral worth and strength of
deed, were undoubtedly to be Mr. Grewgious and Helena
Landless." With this statement I concur. Mr. Walters's one
mistake was that he backed the wrong person, as I purpose to
prove in the remainder of this discussion.

Dick Datchery was none other than Hiram Grewgious.

Who Was Dick Datchery?

(PART TWO)

DICK DATCHERY was none other than Hiram Grewgious. I realize that when I make this assertion I am going contrary to the opinions expressed by all the writers who have previously dealt with this topic. But the belief that Grewgious is Datchery has been growing on me for more than three years. For a long time I hesitated to express my belief in writing, but at last the conviction that I had something new to contribute to the Datchery problem impelled me to set down my ideas on paper. My conviction was later strengthened by a startling discovery I made while rereading the most fascinating of mysteries. What this discovery is, must be withheld until I reach the end of this study. At present I have the heavy burden of bringing forward proof to establish the validity of my contention. This I shall do to the best of my ability, letting the reader judge of its worth.

What sort of person was the man whom I assert to be Dick Datchery, the white-haired stranger who suddenly appeared in Cloisterham? Dickens presents him to us in the ninth chapter of the novel, when he comes to visit Rosa at the Nuns' House. His description of the old lawyer is striking and unforgettable. "Mr. Grewgious had been well selected for his trust, as a man of incorruptible integrity, but certainly for no other appropriate quality discernible on the surface. He was an arid, sandy man, who, if he had been put

into a grinding mill, looked as if he would have ground immediately into high-dried snuff. He had a scanty flat crop of hair, in
colour and consistency like some very mangy yellow fur tippet; it
was so unlike hair, that it must have been a wig, but for the stupendous improbability of anybody's voluntarily sporting such a
head. The little play of feature that his face presented, was cut deep
into it, in a few hard curves that made it more like work; and he
had certain notches in his forehead, which looked as though Nature
had been about to touch them into sensibility or refinement, when
she had impatiently thrown away the chisel, and said: 'I really
cannot be worried to finish off this man; let him go as he is.'

"With too great length of throat at his upper end, and too much
ankle-bone and heel at his lower; with an awkward and hesitating
manner; with a shambling walk; and with what is called a near
sight—which perhaps prevented his observing how much white
cotton stocking he displayed to the public eye, in contrast with his
black suit—Mr. Grewgious still had some strange capacity in him
of making on the whole an agreeable impression."

One cannot fail to note the importance of the outstanding moral
quality possessed by Mr. Grewgious: his absolute integrity. Dickens
gives it a position of some prominence. Then he proceeds to the
physical aspects of the man, permitting the reader to infer that the
lawyer's scanty flat crop of hair is admirably suited for the wearing
of a wig. Indeed, the word "wig" is mentioned almost immediately,
though not with the striking force which the sentence containing
it will reveal later. The too great length of throat and the too much
ankle-bone and heel are preparations for Mr. Grewgious's often
repeated reference to himself as an "angular person." The awkward
and hesitating manner, the shambling walk, and the nearsighted-
ness are characteristics which I suspect are legitimately introduced
by Dickens for the express purpose of leading the reader astray. At
this point in the novel, Dickens would hardly want to depict Grewgious as the person whom the reader might readily recall as the most
logical candidate for the part of Datchery. He does, however, play

fair to the extent of saying that the old lawyer's near sight "perhaps" prevented his observing certain grotesque particulars of his attire. And he concludes with the statement that the man "had some strange capacity in him of making on the whole an agreeable impression" despite his apparent awkwardness.

We meet Mr. Grewgious for the second time on a foggy December afternoon when Edwin Drood comes to visit him in his chambers at Staple Inn. It is on this momentous occasion that Mr. Grewgious hands over to Edwin the precious ring of diamonds and rubies.

We learn that Mr. Grewgious had been bred to the Bar and had laid himself out for chamber practice—to draw deeds. Then an arbitration had come his way, in which he had gained great credit "as one indefatigable in seeking out right and doing right." This phrase is of the utmost importance, for the gray-haired stranger who visits Cloisterham is likewise tireless in his efforts to establish justice; he, too, is doing right by tracking down a man whom he suspects of murder.

Mr. Grewgious had at last found his vocation when a receivership was "blown into his pocket." During the period of time in which the events of the story take place, he is a receiver and agent to two wealthy estates—but we must remember that he deputes their legal business to a firm of solicitors on the floor below. As the English critic Mr. George Orwell has so keenly observed, very few of the leading characters created by Dickens work hard at any stated trade or profession; we are not told in detail what they do to earn their daily bread. I believe that we are unusually favored in what we are told of Grewgious, because his legal training is to have significance. At any rate, it may safely be assumed that Mr. Grewgious was a man of some means, for his hospitality in the way of food was generous; he had a closet "usually containing something good to drink"; "and he held some not empty cellarage at the bottom of the common stair." It is not too illogical, then, to suppose that Mr. Grewgious enjoyed a manner of living that permitted him

to be "idle" whenever he so desired. In all these respects he and
Datchery were kindred spirits—for the single buffer living upon his
means was likewise not averse to good fare.

Dickens then tells us, after referring to the accounts and account
books, the files of correspondence, and the several strongboxes with
which the lawyer's rooms were encumbered, that "the apprehension
of dying suddenly, and leaving one fact or one figure with any incompleteness or obscurity attaching to it, would have stretched Mr.
Grewgious stone-dead any day. The largest fidelity to a trust was
the life-blood of the man." Substitute for "one fact or one figure"
the "disappearance of Edwin Drood," and you have the motive for
the activities of Dick Datchery.

Furthermore, in his description of the old lawyer's chamber,
Dickens adds: "There was no luxury in his room. Even its comforts
were limited to its being dry and warm, and having a snug though
faded fireside." In other words, despite his implied ability to provide himself with a more comfortable home, Grewgious prefers to
live in humble surroundings. The same is true of Dick Datchery,
for when he asks the waiter at the Crozier whether a fair lodging
may be found in Cloisterham, he specifies it further as "something
old," "something odd and out of the way; something venerable,
architectural, and inconvenient."

Yes, Hiram Grewgious had the legal training, the strongly developed sense of justice, and the leisure which we associate with
Datchery.

But had he an incentive, a motive powerful enough to draw him
from his secluded chamber in London and send him forth as Dick
Datchery to track down a murderer? It is my contention that he
had; and that his motive, like the one ascribed to Helena Landless
by Mr. Walters, was threefold. After he had given the ring to Edwin
and was left alone with his thoughts, Dickens tells us that he
"walked softly and slowly to and fro, for an hour and more." He
talks to himself, revealing the fact that he loved Rosa's mother "at
a hopeless, speechless distance"; that he still loved her when she

married the man who "struck in" upon him and won her. Here we have the explanation of his apparent lack of ambition, and of the almost Spartan lodgings in which he lives. He had lost the woman he loved. And now he loves Rosa, not only because she has been for years a sacred trust as his ward—and the largest fidelity to a trust in his lifeblood,—but because she is so like her mother. The ring of diamonds and rubies, taken from the dead hand of that mother, has long been a very dear though inanimate symbol of its owner; her daughter is the living symbol keeping her memory green. What did Dickens say about this ring, in a sentence seemingly obscure at first glance, but weighted with profound significance? "Among the mighty store of wonderful chains that are for over forging, day and night, in the vast iron-works of time and circumstance, there was one chain forged in the moment of that small conclusion, riveted to the foundations of heaven and earth, and gifted with invincible force to hold and drag." The "small conclusion" was, of course, Edwin's decision to say nothing about the ring to Rosa, since they had agreed to break their engagement and part as brother and sister. This decision carried with it the implication that Edwin would keep his pledged word and return the ring to Grewgious. But he disappears, and with him vanishes the ring, the only keepsake of the woman Grewgious adored remaining in his possession. Now every chain has several links; is it too much to assume that one of the links of that particular chain "gifted with invincible force to hold and drag" is the old lawyer's desire to recover the ring he prized so highly?

When Rosa, threatened and tormented by Jasper, flees to her guardian for refuge, what is his first reaction, startled as he is by the complete unexpectedness of her arrival?

"He saw her, and he said, in an undertone: 'Good Heaven!'

"Rosa fell upon his neck, with tears, and then he said, returning her embrace:

" 'My child, my child! I thought you were your mother!' "

And later, when Rosa tells him that Jasper has made odious love to her, entreating him to protect not only her but all of those concerned from his evil designs, what is the old lawyer's reply?

" 'I will,' cried Mr. Grewgious, with a sudden rush of amazing energy. 'Damn him!' "

Then, lest this outburst be too revealing of what is to come later, Dickens makes Grewgious continue, in a heroic-comic manner:

> "Confound his politics!
> Frustrate his knavish tricks!
> On Thee his hopes to fix?
> Damn him again!

But it is worth noting that, soon afterward, Dickens refers to the lawyer's vehemence as "most extraordinary."

Grewgious is certain in his own mind that John Jasper is the murderer of Edwin Drood: he has refused to eat with the wretched uncle after the dramatic scene in which Jasper learns, from him, that the murder has been in vain, since Edwin was not to marry Rosa, the innocent cause of the crime. But he is a shrewd enough lawyer to realize that nothing can be proved against Jasper as long as the *corpus delicti* is still missing. Now that Rosa has actually been threatened, he is stirred to such a degree that he will take an active part in clearing up the mystery surrounding the disappearance of the ill-fated youth. By bringing a murderer to justice he will not only remove Rosa from danger and free Neville Landless from the suspicion darkening his life, but perhaps find the ring he treasures so dearly, as well. This is the triple motive which literally drives him to the Datchery assumption.

That he has been considering ways and means to keep Jasper under close personal surveillance is now a reasonable inference, and explains why Bazzard is off duty at the moment. Ostensibly, Grewgious has given his clerk permission to leave so that he may deal with some matter involving "The Thorn of Anxiety." Actually, the old lawyer wants a clear field for the execution of the strategic move he has been planning—with no witnesses to its intimate details. Such an interpretation of events at this point in the novel is borne out by what Grewgious says on the morning following his outburst, during his conference with Rosa in her room at Staple Inn, a conference including Minor Canon Crisparkle. "When one is in a difficulty or at a loss, one never knows in what direction a way out may chance to open. It is a business principle of mine, in such a case, not to close up any direction, but to keep an eye on every direction that may present itself. I could relate an anecdote in point, but that it would be premature." Not to close up any direction—even though it might mean the donning of a wig, the blackening of his sandy eyebrows, and the playing of a difficult role. He has already been turning over in his mind the idea of going in disguise to Cloisterham; he could put this idea into words, but that it would be premature.

Later that same day, after Lieutenant Tartar has been admitted to the group, and after Rosa has met Helena in Tartar's rooms, Miss Landless, greatly worried about her brother, entreats Rosa to seek Mr. Crisparkle's advice in the following terms: "Ask him whether it would be best to wait until any more maligning and pursuing of Neville on the part of this wretch shall disclose itself, or to try to anticipate it: I mean, so far as to find out whether any such goes on darkly about us." The Minor Canon finds it difficult to express an opinion without consulting Grewgious. And what does Dickens tell us about the lawyer's decision? "Mr. Grewgious held decidedly to the general principle, that if you could steal a march upon a brigand or a wild beast, you had better do it; and he also held decidedly to the special case, that John Jasper was a brigand and a wild beast in combination." I believe that is Dickens's way of revealing Grewgious's determination to go to Cloisterham in the guise of Datchery and prove that Jasper is the murderer of his nephew.

Yes, Hiram Grewgious had a powerful motive for the Datchery assumption: love for Rosa's mother and for the daughter who so resembled her; his anxiety to recover the ring; and his promise to Rosa—given in the strongest words we ever hear him utter—that he will protect her and the others involved in Jasper's threat.

Among those others is Neville Landless, fretting under the gen-

eral suspicion that it was he who caused Edwin's death. And we
should not forget Jasper's declaration to Rosa that he will eventually put the hangman's noose about Neville's neck because he
has learned, from statements made by Minor Canon Crisparkle,
that young Landless was his nephew's rival for her love—an inexpiable offense in Jasper's eyes. We must remember also that, six
months after Edwin's disappearance, when the Minor Canon visits
Grewgious in London, we are told that Grewgious has taken an
interest in Neville, and that it was he who recommended the rooms
now occupied by young Landless. And the lawyer is even then keeping a watch over Jasper, who is spying on Neville; his sense of
justice is even then being prompted to a passive form of activity,
although not of so direct a sort as he will display when he tracks
the murderer through the streets of Cloisterham.

Incidentally, we learn something of importance in the course of
this visit, when Grewgious says to the Minor Canon: "If you will
kindly step round here behind me, in the gloom of the room, and
will cast your eye at the second-floor landing window in yonder
house, I think you will hardly fail to see a slinking individual in
whom I recognize our local friend." Excellent powers of vision
indeed have been developed by the man whom Dickens described
earlier as having a "near sight."

If Grewgious has a compelling motive and a carefully laid plan
to go to Cloisterham as Dick Datchery, it must follow inevitably
that we shall find some points of similarity between him and the
white-haired stranger. I maintain that such resemblances do exist,
although Dickens deemed it wise to touch upon them lightly, lest
the average reader's suspicions—if any existed—be roused to such a
degree that they might become convictions. Too sudden or apparent
a revelation would have defeated the novelist's purpose; it would
have destroyed the interest which was to be suspended from Parts
V and VI up to the end. It is no easy task for the writer of a first-rate
mystery story to play fair with the reader without disclosing the
solution of his problem before the moment when it will achieve its

maximum effect. Yet such is the challenge which must be accepted by all who desire to be outstanding exponents of this exacting form of creative writing. Now Dickens not only met the challenge to play fair, but also kept secret the solution of the riddle he had contrived. The hundreds of books and articles written about his last, unfinished novel proclaim that it still remains a real mystery; that its author, although approaching the valley of the shadow of death, was in complete control of his most tightly woven and intricate plot; and that he was developing it with unusual mastery. He made use of every legitimate device to fool the reader, but he did leave subtle indications linking Grewgious with Datchery.

It has already been pointed out that his detailed account of the growth of Grewgious's legal training was not without special intent. A sound knowledge of the law underlying Datchery's method of questioning the persons with whom he came in contact is so evident that Mr. Montagu Saunders thought the gray-haired stranger an entirely new character, a man of sound legal training placed at Grewgious's disposal by the firm of solicitors who handled matters for the old lawyer. Despite the fact that Dickens was not in the habit of introducing fresh characters of importance when halfway through a story, Mr. Saunders is perfectly correct in his recognition of the legal tone of Datchery's questions. When Datchery is sounding that pompous ass, Mayor Thomas Sapsea, for the purpose of learning whether suspicion of foul play in connection with Edwin's disappearance has fallen upon any particular person (he knows full well it has, but is drawing out His Honor to get his reactions), the following delightful exchange of conversation takes place:

" 'But proof, sir, proof must be built up stone by stone,' said the Mayor. 'As I say, the end crowns the work. It is not enough that Justice should be morally certain; she must be immorally certain— legally, that is.'

" 'His Honour,' said Mr. Datchery, 'reminds me of the nature of the law. Immoral. How true!' "

The conceited Sapsea undoubtedly interprets this remark of Datchery's as confirmation of his deep perspicacity; we realize that the gray-haired stranger not only takes the measure of the boastful mayor, but expresses an opinion of the law itself—an opinion born of long experience with its intricacies.

Even in quite simple matters, such as the rental of lodgings, Dickens suggests that both Grewgious and Datchery proceed with the same degree of thoroughness based upon familiarity with the legal aspects of the situation. When Grewgious makes arrangements to settle Rosa and Miss Twinkleton in one of the apartments available in the home of Mrs. Billickin, Dickens tells us: "By this time Mr. Grewgious had his agreement-lines, and his earnest money, ready. 'I have signed it for the ladies, ma'am,' he said, 'and you'll have the goodness to sign it for yourself, Christian and Surname, there, if you please.'" There follows an interlude in the course of which Mrs. Billickin explains most emphatically why she will *not* sign her Christian name, whereupon we read: "Details were then settled for taking possession on the next day but one, when Miss Twinkleton might reasonably be expected." In like manner, Dick Datchery, when he decides to take the rooms offered by Mrs. Tope, the Verger's wife, acts with the same care and does everything in accordance with legality. "He found the rent moderate, and everything as quaintly inconvenient as he could desire. He agreed, therefore, to take the lodging then and there, and money down, possession to be had next evening, on condition that reference was permitted him to Mr. Jasper as occupying the gatehouse, of which on the other side of the gateway, the Verger's hole-in-the-wall was an appanage or subsidary part."

The procedure on the part of both men is the same; it is but one of the many ways in which Dickens has linked them together inevitably.

Since mention has been made of Datchery's lodgings in Cloisterham, it might be well to consider the encouraging words spoken to Rosa by Grewgious when he leaves her at Furnival's on the night of that same torrid day when she fled in terror from Jasper: " 'There is a stout gate of iron bars to keep him out,' said Mr. Grewgious, smiling; 'and Furnival's is fire-proof, and specially watched and lighted, and *I* live over the way!' " It may be mere coincidence, but when Datchery takes up residence at Mrs. Tope's in Cloisterham, he, too, lives "on the other side of the gateway," which was "over the way" from John Jasper.

We have seen how Datchery was accustomed to lounge hatless about the streets of the cathedral city, with his long white hair streaming. Dickens reiterates this tendency not once or twice, but several times. In my earlier discussion of the Datchery disguise, I have already given my interpretation of this insistence on a small detail. Slight as the similarity may be, it is interesting to observe that Grewgious, anxious to provide Rosa with food on the occasion of her flight from Cloisterham, "ran across to Furnival's, without his hat, to give his various directions." It was by no means necessary for Dickens to insert that little touch; it is possible that he did so deliberately.

I have already dealt with Datchery's habit of shaking his hair—a gesture inducing Mr. J. Cuming Walters to the belief that he was really Helena Landless,—and I intimated that he did so because he was obliged to repress a more characteristic mannerism made impossible by reason of the wig he was wearing. What is this gesture but a modification of the lawyer's well-known smoothing action, so often described by Dickens, in so many different ways?

1. "Mr. Grewgious, with a sense of not having managed his opening point quite as neatly as he might have desired, smoothed his head from back to front as if he had just dived, and were pressing the water out—this smoothing action, however superfluous, was habitual with him—and took a pocket-book from his coat-pocket, and a stump of black-lead pencil from his waistcoat-pocket."

2. "Mr. Grewgious pulled off his hat to smooth his head, and, having smoothed it, nodded it contentedly, and put his hat on again."

3. "Mr. Grewgious smoothed his head and face, and stood looking at the fire."

The wig worn by Dick Datchery permits Dickens to kill two birds with one stone: accompanied by this tendency of Datchery's to shake his hair, it subtly suggests what it actually is—while it also serves to conceal the Grewgious smoothing action, modified by necessity. And furthermore, the reader will consider it perfectly natural for a person to shake the long hair of an oppressive wig, especially when the person concerned, whoever he may be, is not accustomed to wearing such an article.

Before the first of the three quotations describing Mr. Grewgious's smoothing habit has been forgotten, mention must be made of the fact that Mr. Datchery, too, carried a pocketbook, and presumably a pencil. Now this point of similarity may well appear puerile in the extreme; yet Dickens seems to emphasize it needlessly with respect to Datchery. When the gray-haired stranger, still in the company of Mayor Sapsea, first beholds the amazing inscription composed by His Honor in memory of his deceased wife and engraved upon her monument, Dickens describes his reactions in the following manner: "Mr. Datchery became so ecstatic over Mr. Sapsea's composition, that, in spite of his intention to end his days in Cloisterham, and therefore his probably having in reserve many opportunities of copying it, he would have transcribed it into his pocket-book on the spot, but for the slouching towards them of its material producer and perpetuator, Durdles, whom Mr. Sapsea hailed, not sorry to show him a bright example of behaviour to superiors."

The pocket-book and pencil naturally call to mind another of the old lawyer's characteristics: that of checking off the various items of a list, real or fancied. Dickens gives us at least three examples of this methodical habit.

1. "Mr. Grewgious smoothed his smooth head again, and then made another reference to his pocket-book; lining out 'well and happy,' as disposed of."

2. " 'I have now, my dear,' he added, blurring out 'Will' with his pencil, 'discharged myself of what is doubtless a formal duty in this case, but still a duty in such a case.' "

3. " 'I am right so far,' said Mr. Grewgious. 'Tick that off'; which he did, with his right thumb on his left."

When he appears in Cloisterham as Dick Datchery, Grewgious translates this checking habit into the old tavern method of keeping score, with a piece of chalk in lieu of a pencil. "At length he rises, throws open the door of a corner cupboard, and refers to a few uncouth chalked strokes on its inner side.—He sighs over the contemplation of its poverty, takes a bit of chalk from one of the cupboard shelves, and pauses with it in his hand, uncertain what addition to make to the account. 'I think a moderate stroke,' he concludes, 'is all I am justified in scoring up'; so, suits the action to the word, closes the cupboard, and goes to bed."

It is amazing to me how the writing down of one similarity between Grewgious and Datchery, illustrated by direct quotations from the text of the novel, almost invariably suggests another. The passage above brings to my mind the tendency of both men to talk aloud when they are alone, and to suit the action to the word, as Dickens so neatly puts it by borrowing Hamlet's phrase. The next two selections are so striking in their parallelism that I shall let them speak for themselves. It is just possible that they may be coincidental in this respect, but I very much doubt it. Dickens, always extremely sensitive to criticism, had been nettled by the accusation that some of his plots were loosely constructed, and that certain of his melodramatic denouements were poorly motivated. He was determined, therefore, that *The Mystery of Edwin Drood* should give the lie to such observations; he was manipulating its intricate problem with the skill of a watchmaker. But let us consider the passages to which I have alluded.

1. "Mr. Grewgious crossed the staircase to his raw and foggy bedroom, and was soon ready for bed. Dimly catching sight of his face in the misty looking-glass, he held his candle to it for a moment.

" 'A likely some one, *you,* to come into anybody's thoughts in such an aspect!' he exclaimed. 'There! there! there! Get to bed, poor man, and cease to jabber!'

"With that, he extinguished his light, pulled up the bedclothes around him, and with another sigh shut out the world."

2. "Said Mr. Datchery to himself that night, as he looked at his white hair in the gas-lighted looking-glass over the coffee-room chimney-piece at the Grozier, and shook it out: 'For a single buffer, of an easy temper, living idly on his means, I have had a rather busy afternoon!' "

I cannot refrain from directing attention to Grewgious's exclamation in the first of the two passages quoted above; it affords a perfectly pat answer to the question: "Who can Dick Datchery possibly be?" "A likely some one, *you,* to come into anybody's thoughts in such an aspect!"

The various writers who have backed one character or another in the novel for the role of Dick Datchery have contended, with but few exceptions, that their candidate talks like the white-haired stranger; they have quoted certain words or phrases not unlike those uttered by Lieutenant Tartar, Helena Landless, and others. There is, then, nothing new about my intention to follow the same sort of procedure. But in doing so I shall limit myself to four points of similarity only, not because there are no others which might be brought forward, but for the sake of brevity. For the same reason, also, I do not propose to multiply the speeches adduced as proofs, nor shall I establish the circumstances in which they were made. They are all taken from the text of the novel, and those who are familiar with it will have no difficulty in recognizing these spot passages, if I may so term them.

First of all, I would point out the tendency displayed by both Grewgious and Datchery for long, sonorous speeches alternating with short, pithy ones. The inclination to speak at some length is more marked in Grewgious, for he is often the dominating personality by reason of the situation in which he appears; he is therefore in a position to have his say according to his pleasure. When he goes about Cloisterham as Dick Datchery, the lawyer is not so prone to talk in round periods—although he does so on occasion. Illustrations of both styles follow.

DATCHERY

1. "Let him be! Don't you see you have lamed him?"
"Come here."
"Stay there, then, and show me which is Mr. Tope's."
"Show me where it is, and I'll give you something."
"That's Tope's?"
"Indeed?"
"Why not,"

2. "Might I ask His Honour whether that gentleman we have just left is the gentleman of whom I have heard in the neighbourhood as being much afflicted by the loss of a nephew, and concentrating his life on avenging the loss?"

"The Worshipful the Mayor gives them a character of which they may indeed be proud. I would ask His Honour (if I might be permitted) whether there are not many objects of great interest in the city which is under his beneficent sway?"

GREWGIOUS

1. " 'Yes,' said Mr. Grewgious, 'I refer it to you, as an authority.' "
" 'Likely so,' assented Mr. Grewgious, 'likely so. I am a hard man in the grain.' "
"No to be sure; he *may* not."
" 'His responsibility is very great, though,' said Mr. Grewgious at length, with his eyes on the fire."
" 'And let him be sure that he trifles with no one,' said Mr. Grewgious; 'neither with himself, nor with any other.' "

2. " 'Mr. Edwin will correct it where it's wrong,' resumed Mr. Grewgious, 'and will throw in a few touches from the life. I dare say it is wrong in many particulars, and wants many touches from the life, for I was born a Chip, and have neither soft sympathies nor soft experiences. Well! I hazard the guess that the true lover's mind is completely permeated by the beloved object of his affections. I hazard the guess that her dear name is precious to him, cannot be heard or repeated without emotion, and is preserved sacred. If he has any distinguishing appelation of fondness for her, it is reserved for her, and is not for common ears. A name that it would be a privilegé to call her by, being alone with her own bright self, it would be a liberty, a coldness, an insensibility, almost a breach of good faith, to flaunt elsewhere.' "

The habit of repeating themselves is common to both Grewgious and Datchery, as may be seen even in the passages just quoted for a totally different purpose. Not only single words, but whole phrases, are reiterated by the two men. As one might expect, the tendencies under discussion are more pronounced in Grewgious; Dickens did not want to make the similarities between them too apparent, for interest would be gone if the reader were able to deduce almost immediately that the lawyer and the gray-haired stranger were one and the same person. But Datchery is certainly an echo, albeit a faint one, of his *alter ego*.

DATCHERY

"Good. See here. You owe me half of this."

"I tell you you owe me half of this, because I have no sixpence in my pocket. So the next time you meet me you shall do something else for me, to pay me."

"His Honour the Mayor does me too much credit."

"Again, His Honour the Mayor does me too much credit."

"His Honour reminds me of the nature of the law. Immoral. How true!"

"How forcible!—And yet, again, how true!"

In order to conserve space, I shall merely add that in his conversation with Thomas Sapsea, Datchery addresses the worthy gentleman as "The Worshipful the Mayor" twice; as "His Honour the Mayor" six times; and as "His Honour" no less than eight times.

GREWGIOUS

"My dear, how do you do? I am glad to see you. My dear, how much improved you are. Permit me to hand you a chair, my dear."

" 'Not at all, I thank you,' answered Mr. Grewgious."

" 'Not at all, I thank you,' answered Mr. Grewgious again."

" 'I couldn't get a morsel down my throat, I thank you,' answered Mr. Grewgious."

Interjections suggestive of either a meditative frame of mind or a clearing of the throat to attract attention are used by both men. The "Umps!" employed by Mr. Grewgious on at least two occasions is quite naturally not discoverable in anything that Datchery says; such an unusual exclamation, had it been voiced by Datchery, would have given away the whole show.

GREWGIOUS

" 'Marriage.' Hem!"

" 'Hem! Permit me, sir, to have the honour,' said Mr. Grewgious, advancing with extended hand, 'for an honour I truly esteem it.' "

DATCHERY

"Hum; ha! A very small score this; a very poor score!"

What I may call a deprecatory or belittling note is sounded in the speeches of both men. It is an outstanding characteristic of Grewgious, who seems reluctant to attribute to himself any of the qualities of which the average individual so frequently boasts. When he has to put himself forward as Datchery in Cloisterham, Grewgious is in no position to indulge this habitual understatement of his virtues, of which he has a great many. It may have been with full knowledge and intent that Dickens gave him the name "Hiram," which means "noble." But this Grewgious characteristic does crop up in Datchery on at least one occasion.

GREWGIOUS

" 'I made,' he said, turning the leaves: 'I made a guiding memorandum or so—as I usually do, for I have no conversational powers whatever—to which I will, with your permission, my dear, refer.' "

" 'And May!' pursued Mr. Grewgious—'I am not at liberty to be definite— May!—my conversational powers are so very limited that I know I shall not come well out of this—May!—it ought to be put imaginatively, but I have no imagination—May!—the thorn of anxiety is as nearly the mark as I am likely to get—May it come out at last!' "

DATCHERY

"I beg pardon. A selfish precaution on my part, and not personally interesting to anybody but myself. But as a buffer living on his means, and having an idea of doing it in this lovely place in peace and quiet, for remaining span of life, I beg to ask if the Tope family are quite respectable?"

I submit that the speeches presented to the reader, especially those so strikingly marked by repetition of the same words and phrases, were uttered by one and the same man.

And now I come at last to the discovery made one night while I was pondering over certain parts of the book which I have had before my eyes as often as any other that I can recall. I would not venture to guess how many times I have compared the descriptions of Mr. Grewgious and Dick Datchery, but I can say with assurance that they have been by no means few. Both men are so familiar to me as the result of constant rereading of what they are like and what they say that they seem like old friends who tend to be taken for granted—and are so taken far too often. I was well along in my manuscript when I turned again to Dickens's portrayal of the two characters in whom I have been so deeply interested. But I did so on this occasion with a result which was as startling as it was unforeseen. There on the pages blackened by notes and heavy underscorings I saw what had never appeared before. Reluctant as I am to use such a word to sum up my experience, it was nothing less than a revelation.

What I perceived with instantaneous awareness on the part of the mind's eye, to borrow Hamlet's felicitous expression for something like an inward vision, was the transparent possibility of so rearranging certain parts of the Grewgious and Datchery descriptions as to make the link between the two men a certainty. I make this statement advisedly, for I cannot conceive of such a rearrangement as resulting from mere chance. I am no mathematician, but I doubt that the probability of its so doing could be expressed by any figures short of those we are wont to term astronomical.

In order to make clear to the reader what I saw, I must first set down a part of Dickens's description of Dick Datchery, and then place after it a portion of the description of Mr. Grewgious.

DATCHERY: "This gentleman's white head was unusually large, and his shock of white hair was unusually ample."

GREWGIOUS: "He had a scanty flat crop of hair, in colour and consistency like some very mangy yellow fur tippet; it was so unlike hair, that it must have been a wig, but for the stupendous improbability of anybody's voluntarily sporting such a head."

And now for the rearrangement, which records for the first time, to the best of my knowledge, an entirely new sentence.

This gentleman's white head was unusually large, and his shock of white hair was unusually ample; it was so unlike hair, that it must have been a wig, but for the stupendous improbability of anybody's voluntarily sporting such a head.

Is that sentence, perfect in its grammatical construction, punctuation, and significance, the result of pure coincidence or blind chance? I cannot believe so; it is my firm conviction that the juxta-position I have effected was deliberately made possible by Charles Dickens himself. Mark well the adjective with which the author qualifies so strongly the word "improbability"—"stupendous." Yes, here indeed is the stupendous improbability—the climax of that interest which was to be kept suspended from Parts V and VI of *The Mystery of Edwin Drood* until the end: Hiram Grewgious *is* Dick Datchery. The two, through the demonstrable intermingling of the descriptions Dickens gave them, are made one.

Whether the readers of this study will find my composite a legitimate argument in favor of my contention that Grewgious and Datchery are one and the same person, I do not know. They must judge for themselves the validity of the device which has impressed me deeply. Meanwhile, with all the courage of my convictions, I give them Hiram Grewgious, alias Dick Datchery, the mysterious white-haired stranger of Cloisterham.

John Jasper—
Murderer

Ａ ND YET he was so terrible a man! In short, the poor girl (for what could she know of the criminal intellect, which its own professed students perpetually misread, because they persist in trying to reconcile it with the average intellect of average men, instead of identifying it as a horrible wonder apart) could get by no road to any other conclusion than that he *was* a terrible man, and must be fled from.

⬦ ⬦ ⬦

This terrible man first appears in the opening chapter of *The Mystery of Edwin Drood,* Dickens's last, unfinished novel. By reason of its contrast between the sordid opium den in Shadwell and the quiet cathedral in the city of Cloisterham—a contrast as antipodal as the opposition of light and shadow in a novel by Hugo—the chapter is one of the most startling in English literature. It strikes the same prophetic note of things to come which is sounded in the witches' scene heralding the tragedy of *Macbeth.* It typifies the eternal contest between good and evil; it reveals in Jasper— though yet unnamed—a man suffering from an abnormal state of mind, from a psychosis aggravated by drug intoxication.

The motive driving this man to murder is already present in the opium-induced dream from which he is recovering. Jasper is the Sultan; Edwin Drood, his nephew, is the robber; Rosa Bud— the object of his passion—is the dancing girl whom Edwin has stolen from him. And the ancient English cathedral tower represents the Victorian morality and society against which Jasper is a rebel.

The method he will use to commit the murder of which he dreams is foreshadowed when he seizes a Chinaman "with both hands by the throat"; it is the method of the strangler. And the man emerging from his opium debauch seems to fear that he has talked; that he has revealed in his drugged stupor the plan which he is already formulating in his brain, that "horrible wonder apart."

Here, then, is a potential murderer dramatically presented at the very outset of the novel. There is no doubt that Dickens meant to give us a study of such a man—a study which in its psychological implications was to go far beyond any of a similar nature he had previously made.

The "jaded traveller" returns to Cloisterham and its cathedral to take part in the vesper service. And here Dickens brings in a motif destined to be profoundly significant in the later development of the novel, and about which I shall have more to say. "Then, the Sacristan locks the iron-barred gates that divide the sanctuary from the chancel, and all of the procession having scuttled into their places, hide their faces; and then the intoned words, 'WHEN THE WICKED MAN—' rise among groins of arches and beams of roof, awakening muttered thunder."

Note that Dickens puts the intoned words in capitals, thus stressing their importance. They are from Ezekiel, 18:27: "Again, when the wicked man turneth away from his wickedness that he hath committed, and doeth that which is lawful and right, he shall save his soul alive." That is the Law and the Prophet; how is Jasper to meet them?

In the second chapter, we learn from Mr. Tope, the Verger, that Jasper has seizures. During the service he had "a kind of fit on him after a little. His memory grew DAZED." This information is not surprising, considering the recent orgy during which he had smoked at least five pipefuls of opium. Opium undermines the will power and causes psychosis; in Jasper's case, a psychosis not unlike paraphrenia, that exuberant development in the victim's mind of fantastic delusions and hallucinations which yet allow his person-

ality so to preserve itself that it can make normal reactions to social
life on occasion.

What sort of man is the physical Jasper, as the inhabitants of
Cloisterham know him? "Mr. Jasper is a dark man of some six-and-
twenty, with thick, lustrous, well-arranged black hair and whiskers.
He looks older than he is, as dark men often do. His voice is deep
and good, his face and figure are good, his manner is a little sombre."
He plays the piano, sings well, is a successful teacher of music, and
is a reader—witness "the book-shelves on the wall."

He is young Edwin Drood's uncle and guardian, undoubtedly a
younger brother of Edwin's mother. He is apparently devoted to
Edwin, for whom he shows an almost womanish solicitation. When
his nephew comes to visit him, he addresses the youth as "My dear
Edwin!" and continues: "Get off your greatcoat, bright boy, and
sit down here in your own corner. Your feet are not wet? Pull your
boots off. Do pull your boots off." He makes frequent use of endear-
ing terms, and is not averse to touching the object of his affection.

Nevertheless, "once for all, a look of intentness and intensity—a
look of hungry, exacting, watchful, and yet devoted affection—is
always, now and ever afterwards, on the Jasper face." "It is always
concentrated." Dickens expresses himself in this way to show the
conflict going on in Jasper's mind. He envies Edwin his carefree
life; he is genuinely fond of his nephew, but the fact that Edwin is
to marry Rosa has doomed him to destruction.

Jasper has an unusual capacity for seeing things not within his
range of vision. "Fixed as the look the young fellow meets, is, there
is yet in it some strange power of suddenly including the sketch
over the chimney piece." This sketch is Edwin's portrait of Rosa
Bud, to whom he has been pledged since childhood—the young girl
to whom Jasper gives music lessons and whom he loves with a
secret passion.

When Edwin rebels against marriage by anticipation and a life
"laid down to scale, and lined and dotted out—like a surveyor's
plan," Jasper has another seizure and confesses to Edwin that he

has been taking opium for a pain. That he is Lay Precentor of the cathedral, choirmaster, and music master, means nothing to him; he hates the cramped monotony of his existence. He is weary of the religious service. He bursts out against the cathedral, which is to him the epitome of the "oppressive respectability" of Cloisterham itself. "No wretched monk who droned his life away in that gloomy place, before me, can have been more tired of it than I am. He could take for relief (and did take) to carving demons out of the stalls and seats and desks. What shall I do? Must I take to carving them out of my heart?"

But this is a confidence between them. "I have reposed it in you, because—" He breaks off, for he has been on the verge of saying: "because we both love Rosa." And he finally concludes, with reference to his self-revelation: "Take it as a warning, then."

This speech has a double meaning; it not only admonishes Edwin that he should subdue himself to his vocation, as Jasper has resolved to do, but it reveals the intent to destroy Edwin, who stands between Jasper and Rosa. And "Mr. Jasper's steadiness of face and figure becomes so marvellous that his breathing seems to have stopped" until Edwin, who is essentially selfish, assures him that he was not prepared for such sacrifice—owing to fondness for him—as the laying bare of his uncle's inner self.

Edwin has no idea that Jasper loves Rosa; he has missed the deeper, hidden meaning of the warning.

"You won't be warned, then?" Jasper reiterates, with a quiet smile.

"No, Jack."

"You can't be warned, then?"

Thus Jasper makes doubly sure that Edwin has not taken his confidence for the personal threat it really is, since the intent to murder his nephew already occupies his mind.

In his notes for this chapter in which Jasper and Edwin dine together and hold the conversation which I have summarized, Dickens wrote: "Uncle and Nephew. Murder very far off." But the germ of murder lay in that "horrible wonder apart," and we may expect to see it develop at our next meeting with Jasper. It is late autumn when he is received for the first time by the pompous ass, Thomas Sapsea; certainly before November 9, Lord Mayor's Day, for Sapsea has not yet been exalted to the office of mayor, a position he later holds. Jasper has come—evidently at the invitation of the older man—to speak about the late Mrs. Sapsea, and to give his opinion of the amazing epitaph which the widower has composed in her honor. His real purpose in coming is to flatter Sapsea, because he plans to make use of him later on. Or rather, Dickens intends him to make use of Sapsea, for again in the notes written for his own guidance we find: "MR. SAPSEA. Connect Jasper with him. (He will want a solemn donkey by and by.)"

Jasper certainly does flatter Sapsea, and he meets old Durdles, the stonemason, of whom Dickens says: "With the Cathedral crypt he is better acquainted than any living authority." Durdles has also been summoned by Sapsea in connection with the epitaph. Sapsea gives him the composition—approved by Jasper,—whereupon ensues a conversation which is of paramount importance to the choirmaster.

"Is this to be put in hand at once, Mr. Sapsea?" Durdles inquires.

"Mr. Sapsea, with an Author's anxiety to rush into publication, replies that it cannot be out of hand too soon.

" 'You had better let me have the key then,' says Durdles.

" 'Why, man, it is not to be put *inside the monument!*' "

The italics are mine—for it is my contention that Jasper first conceives the idea of secreting Edwin's body in this particular tomb as a result of Sapsea's remark.

Sapsea gets the key to the monument and hands it to Durdles, who tucks it away in a large, inside breast pocket of his flannel coat. Whereupon Jasper remarks: "Why, Durdles! you are undermined with pockets!"

" 'And I carries weight in 'em too, Mr. Jasper. Feel those!' producing two other large keys.

" 'Hand me Mr. Sapsea's likewise. Surely this is the heaviest of the three.' "

While Jasper chats with Durdles about the origin of the latter's nickname, "Stony," he has an opportunity to weigh the three keys and become familiar with their appearance. He clinks one key against another, and clinks again with a change of keys. The only purpose of this scene is to inform the reader that Jasper is now cognizant of the shape, weight, and ringing tone of the key to the Sapsea tomb. And we may be sure that he notes the fact that Durdles "drops his two keys back into his pocket one by one, and buttons them up"; that he "takes his dinner-bundle from the chair-back on which he hung it when he came in"; and that he "distributes the weight he carries, by tying the third key up in it." Can there be any doubt that Dickens meant this "third key" to be that of the Sapsea monument? Jasper has indeed obtained a great deal of satisfaction from his visit, for his plan to rid himself of his nephew is now definitely beginning to take shape.

Jasper next appears at the "friendly dinner" planned by Minor Canon Crisparkle and his mother to welcome the advent of Neville and Helena Landless to Cloisterham, a dinner which also brings together as guests Edwin and Rosa, Miss Twinkleton—headmistress of the Nuns' House, the school in which Rosa is a pupil and to which Helena is soon to be admitted,—and Luke Honeythunder, blustering philanthropist and guardian of the newcomers. The dinner is a "doleful breakdown," owing to Luke's bumptious arrogance,— but the confidences which follow are of great significance for Jasper. Then comes the piano scene, during which Jasper accompanies Rosa as she sings, and displays powers of animal magnetism or hypnosis which reveal a new phase of his complex nature.

"It was a consequence of his playing the accompaniment without notes, and of her being a heedless little creature, very apt to go wrong, that he followed her lips most attentively, with his eyes as well as hands; carefully and softly hinting the key-note from time to time." And not content with this suggestion of Jasper's dominance of Rosa, Dickens soon adds: "As Jasper watched the pretty lips, and ever and again hinted the one note, as though it were a low whisper from himself, the voice became less steady, until all at once the singer broke into a burst of tears, and shrieked out, with her hands over her eyes: 'I can't bear this! I am frightened! Take me away!' "

Miss Landless, who is herself possessed of hypnotic and telepathic powers, at once takes charge of Rosa, while Jasper sits quiet, "not even looking round." Edwin, with his usual obtuseness, remarks: "Pussy's not used to an audience; that's the fact. She got nervous, and couldn't hold out. Besides, Jack, you are such a conscientious master, and require so much, that I believe you make her afraid of you. No wonder."

"No wonder," repeats Helena. But with deeper insight into the cause of Rosa's breakdown.

"There, Jack, you hear? You would be afraid of him, under similar circumstances, wouldn't you, Miss Landless?"

"Not under any circumstances," returns Helena.

"Jasper brought down his hands, looked over his shoulder, and begged to thank Miss Landless for her vindication of his character. Then he fell to dumbly playing, without striking the notes, while his little pupil was taken to an open window for air, and was otherwise petted and restored. When she was brought back, his place was empty."

He recognizes in Helena Landless a powerful adversary, one who can get the better of him at his own game.

Added meaning is given to this strange scene by Rosa herself, when, in the safety of their bedroom at Miss Twinkleton's school, she makes a confidante of Helena. After telling her new friend that she feels as though Jasper "could pass in through the wall when he is spoken of," she adds: "He has made a slave of me with his looks. He has forced me to understand him, without his saying a word; and he has forced me to keep silence, without his uttering a threat. When I play, he never moves his eyes from my hands. When I sing, he never moves his eyes from my lips. When he cor-

rects me, and strikes a note, or a chord, or plays a passage, he himself is in the sounds, whispering that he pursues me as a lover, and
commanding me to keep his secret. I avoid his eyes, but he forces
me to see them without looking at them. Even when a glaze comes
over them (which is sometimes the case), and he seems to wander
away into a frightful sort of dream in which he threatens most, he
obliges me to know it, and to know that he is sitting close at my side,
more terrible to me than ever."

This is Jasper's hypnotic power exercising the same sort of fascination a snake has over a bird. And Rosa, frightened by this force,
appeals to Helena for protection. It is tacitly given, and Dickens
cannot refrain from a bit of foreshadowing which must inevitably
arouse the reader's interest. "There was a slumbering gleam of fire
in the intense dark eyes [Helena's], though they were then softened
with compassion and admiration. Let whomsoever it most concerned look well to it!" It is not my purpose in this study to deal
with possible plot developments beyond the fragment left by
Dickens, so I shall pass over this foreshadowing. The important part
of Rosa's speech is that final sentence in which she acknowledges
a shadowy presentiment that Jasper is threatening something fearful
in the vague dream into which he seems to wander. That threat is,
of course, the destruction of Edwin.

Circumstances further favor Jasper when he overhears the quarrel
between Edwin and Neville as they leave the Nuns' House after
escorting Rosa and Helena home. This quarrel grows out of
Neville's sudden interest in Rosa and his resentment at Edwin's
patronizing attitude toward his fiancée. That he has overheard the
dispute is an inevitable conclusion, in view of what occurs later at
the gatehouse when he invites them in to his lodgings to take a
stirrup cup after having temporarily composed their differences.
Being quick to perceive that Neville Landless has formed a dislike
for Edwin, he resolves to make the most of it.

His first action upon entering his rooms is to direct attention to
Edwin's portrait of Rosa by shading a lamp to throw the light upon

it, and by asking Neville whether he recognizes it. The ensuing
conversation brings out again Edwin's patronage and indifference
to Rosa, and arouses the antagonism of the impetuous Neville.
Jasper smiles slightly, and turns away to mix a jug of mulled wine
at the fire. When Dickens says, "It seems to require much mixing
and compounding," he is informing the reader that Jasper drugs
the concoction.

The young men continue their quarrel until Jasper hands each
one of them a large goblet glass of his mixture, fills one for himself,
and proposes: "Come, Mr. Neville, we are to drink to my nephew,
Ned. As it is his foot that is in the stirrup—metaphorically—our
stirrup-cup is to be devoted to him. Ned, my dearest fellow, my
love!"

The three men drink, whereupon Jasper deliberately sets out to
foment the antagonism existing between his guests and to bring it
to a pitch of violence.

"Look at him," Jasper cries to young Landless. "See where he
lounges so easily, Mr. Neville! The world is all before him where
to choose. A life of stirring work and interest, a life of change and
excitement, a life of domestic ease and love! Look at him!"

The drugged wine is already having its effect on the two young
men as Jasper proceeds. Needless to say, his own goblet contains
liquid which is free from the drug.

"See how little he heeds it all! It is hardly worth his while to pluck
the golden fruit that hangs ripe on the tree for him. And yet consider the contrast, Mr. Neville. You and I have no prospect of stirring work and interest, or of change and excitement, or of domestic
ease and love. You and I have no prospect (unless you are more
fortunate than I am, which may easily be), but the tedious unchang-
ing round of this dull place."

Jasper speaks from the heart, despite his bantering vein; his envy
of Edwin and his passion for Rosa are the driving motives for what
he says. The desired result is produced; the two young men soon
resume their heated words until both become insulting.

"You are a common fellow, and a common boaster," Neville finally cries.

"Pooh, pooh," returns Edwin, "how should you know? You may know a black common fellow, or a black common boaster, when you see him (and no doubt you have a large acquaintance that way), but you are no judge of white men."

The allusion is to Neville's swarthy skin; he and his twin sister Helena are from Ceylon. Neville flings the dregs of his goblet at Edwin, and is about to hurl the goblet itself when Jasper seizes his arm.

" 'Ned, my dear fellow!' he cries in a loud voice; 'I entreat you, I command you, to be still! Mr. Neville, for shame! Give this glass to me. Open your hand, sir. I WILL have it!' "

Neville throws him off, dashes the goblet down under the grate, and leaves the house, forgetting his hat.

Jasper has gained his end, for he has established a state of hostility between the two, and has in young Landless a potential suspect as the murderer of Edwin when his plan to destroy his nephew has been fully matured and carried out.

To further this situation, Jasper goes to the home of Mr. Crisparkle on the pretext of returning Neville's hat. The good Minor Canon has just seen Neville to bed after a distressing interview. He receives Jasper, and there follows a talk between them which presents one of the most baffling mysteries in the novel. Before I go into this mystery, I must turn back to a previous point in the story, the close of the doleful dinner given by Mr. Crisparkle earlier the same evening.

When Mr. Crisparkle and Neville were returning from seeing Mr. Honeythunder off on the omnibus, the Minor Canon's young charge took occasion to speak of Helena and of himself. He praised his sister in no uncertain terms, but spoke frankly of his own shortcomings resulting from the life he has led.

"And to finish with, sir," he said, "I have been brought up among abject and servile dependents, of an inferior race, and I may easily have contracted some affinity with them. *Sometimes, I don't know but that it may be a drop of what is tigerish in their blood."* The italics are mine.

Later that same evening, when he is endeavoring to explain his apparently intoxicated condition to Mr. Crisparkle after his quarrel with Edwin, Neville says, with reference to young Drood: "He goaded me, sir, beyond my power of endurance. I cannot say whether or no he meant it at first, but he did it. He certainly meant it at last. In short, sir, in the passion into which he lashed me, *I would have cut him down if I could,* and I tried to do it." Again the italics are mine.

Now it is worth noting that on these two occasions Jasper could not conceivably have overheard what Neville said. On the first, he was still at the dinner table in the Crisparkle home, and then at the piano accompanying Rosa. On the second, he was on his way to the Minor Canon's house; his knock at the door is not heard by Crisparkle until he descends the stairs after saying good night to Neville. Yet mark what follows, when Jasper is admitted by the Minor Canon.

" 'We have had an awful scene with him,' says Jasper, in a low voice." He refers, of course, to Neville.

" 'Has it been so bad as that?'

" 'Murderous!'

"Mr. Crisparkle remonstrates: 'No, no, no. Do not use such strong words.'

" 'He might have laid my dear boy dead at my feet. It is no fault of his, that he did not. But that I was, through the mercy of God, swift and strong with him, he would have cut him down on my hearth.'

"The phrase smites home. 'Ah!' thinks Mr. Crisparkle, 'his own words!'

" 'Seeing what I have seen to-night, and hearing what I have heard,' adds Jasper, with great earnestness, 'I shall never know peace of mind when there is danger of those two coming together, with no one else to interfere. It was horrible. There is something of the tiger in his dark blood.'

" 'Ah!' thinks Mr. Crisparkle, 'so he said!' "

How was Jasper aware of the strong statements made by Neville at two widely separated times, and in places at which Jasper could not conceivably have been present? I repeat that we have here one of the outstanding mysteries of the novel. That Dickens considered this enigma a matter of importance, we cannot doubt, for he has so labored the point that it cannot be overlooked or forgotten. One might be tempted to consider it an example of thought transference or reading of the mind, yet Jasper displays no such ability later on in the story, when it would have been to his utmost advantage to do so. What use Dickens would have made of this uncanny knowledge of Jasper's is a matter for conjecture, for I have never as yet seen any discussion of the point I have raised; but the weird, almost verbatim repetition of Neville's remarks certainly impresses me, as it did Mr. Crisparkle, and I cannot pass over it in silence.

As so often happens, the solution of this problem, once it is subjected to careful study, proves surprisingly simple. Mr. Vincent Starrett speaks no more than the truth when he says,[1] "A vast deal of ingenuity has gone into the making of the several solutions to *Edwin Drood;* and it may be that most of them are *too ingenious.*" Certainly I have on occasion been inclined to read into the problem far more than it actually contains, and had I attempted a solution at such times, it would undoubtedly have been more ingenious than the one I now present. And again, as so often happens, much of my difficulty in connection with this whole matter was due to my inadequate analysis of the novel's text.

Dickens himself gives us the clue to the simple solution of the problem when he makes Jasper say to Crisparkle: "... hearing what I have heard": it is the ancient, though reprehensible, habit of eavesdropping that explains the entire situation. And yet the novelist

---

[1] *The Mystery of Edwin Drood,* ed. Vincent Starrett (New York: Heritage Press, 1941), Introduction.

handles and develops it with such skill that he has succeeded for many years in mystifying his readers.

Even after I had reached the conclusion that Jasper had over-heard the striking statements made by Neville Landless, I almost came a cropper because of Dickens's great skill in manipulating the delicate strands of his intricate plot. Having subjected the text of the novel to close scrutiny, I had decided that, while Neville and Crisparkle were returning from seeing Luke Honeythunder off on the omnibus, and while the former was confiding in his tutor-to-be, Jasper was on his way to the gatehouse to fetch some of the music which he and Rosa had studied together. The striking piano scene following the prolonged talk between young Landless and the Minor Canon certainly justified the supposition that, once the din-ner given in honor of the Landless twins was over, some suggestion had been made that Rosa sing for the company then assembled in the Minor Canon's drawing room. Now it was scarcely logical to suppose that either Jasper or Rosa had come to the dinner already prepared for this eventuality—that one or the other had brought a portfolio containing, among other items, the "sorrowful strain of parting" which Rosa was later to sing. It seemed altogether likely that Jasper had been obliged to return to his rooms in the gatehouse to fetch it. Returning, he had come upon Neville and Crisparkle, had lurked behind them, and all unbeknown to them—and to the reader—had overheard much of what they were saying. Such, in essence, was my argument.

Now there would have been ample time for Jasper to have done this. He could easily have gone from Crisparkle's to the gatehouse and have returned before the Minor Canon and Neville came upon the piano scene. And the choirmaster would have heard not only Neville's self-denunciation but also the crucial words, "I don't know but that it may be a drop of what is tigerish in their blood." Dickens himself made such a supposition both possible and plausible, for, after the speech had been made by Neville to Crisparkle, the novelist wrote: "They were now standing at his [the Minor Canon's] house-door, and a cheerful sound of voices and laughter was heard within." Surely this statement makes it inferable that Rosa had not yet begun to sing to Jasper's accompaniment. Furthermore, Crisparkle and Neville take two additional "turns" after this; in the course of the second, the Minor Canon explains to Neville what he knows of the story of Rosa's betrothal to Edwin. Jasper has had plenty of time, therefore, to return from the gatehouse to Crisparkle's drawing room and to be in the midst of his accompaniment of Rosa's song when the Minor Canon and Neville enter.

Reasoning thus, I felt certain that I had within my grasp the first half of a final solution to the problem, when Dickens himself put an insurmountable obstacle in my path. To my dismay, the novelist's statement concerning Jasper, "It was a consequence of his playing the accompaniment *without notes* [the italics are mine]— that he followed her lips most attentively, with his eyes as well as his hands," at once invalidated my whole argument. Clearly the choirmaster had *not* gone to his rooms to fetch any music. And even though Rosa was, in the words of the novelist, "a heedless little creature, very apt to go wrong," she *did* know this "sorrowful strain of parting," and was singing the song from memory. The phrase "without notes" could only mean that Jasper had had no valid reason to go to the gatehouse, that he had not gone, and that he could not possibly have overheard Neville's reference to "abject and servile dependents" and to what was "tigerish in their blood."

And yet I was on the right track, after all; for notwithstanding the complete destruction of the first half of the solution I had evolved, the final answer to the problem was still to be found in Jasper's habit of eavesdropping. Dickens, as I soon discovered, had obligingly suggested the mechanics employed by Jasper in the practice of his undeniable propensity by the simple yet ingenious introduction of a repetition—but a repetition that came subtly, albeit clearly, only after the novelist had previously and successfully mystified his readers.

It will be remembered that Neville, after his heated quarrel with
Edwin in Jasper's rooms, goes hatless "to Minor Canon Corner,
and knocks softly at the door." Mr. Crisparkle, who was then engaged in "very softly touching his piano and practising his favourite
parts in concerted vocal music," is nevertheless quick to hear
Neville's soft knock, and answers it, "candle in hand." He subse-
quently escorts Neville to his "little book-room," and undoubtedly
carries the candle in with him, since no other source of illumination
is even mentioned.

Now once he has got Edwin Drood to bed, Jasper goes to the
Minor Canon's house for the ostensible purpose of returning
Neville's hat, although his real reason for the visit is to impress
upon the Minor Canon the murderous nature of young Landless.
The choirmaster has had plenty of time to come up behind Neville
and to see him admitted by Mr. Crisparkle. For Neville, after the
quarrel and his departure from Jasper's rooms, has stood "in the
midst of a blood-red whirl," and has then staggered away, to spend
some time in the contemplation of suicide, until the thoughts of
self-immolation are driven away by "remembrance of his sister"
and "of what he owes to the good man who has but that very day
won his confidence." And so at last "he repairs to Minor Canon
Corner."

I can see Jasper following him and watching his admittance to
Mr. Crisparkle's house. Undoubtedly familiar with the Minor
Canon's abode, wherein he was a frequent visitor, the choirmaster
goes to the book-room window as soon as he sees the candlelight
shining there through the curtains. He gets his ear as close to the
window as possible. Perhaps he hears at first only a low murmur
of voices, as Neville accuses himself of having begun "dreadfully
ill," and the Minor Canon reproaches his young charge with not
being sober.

But soon Neville Landless becomes heated in his self-defense;
his voice is inevitably pitched in a higher key when he declares:
"We quarreled, sir. He insulted me most grossly. *He had heated*

that tigerish blood I told you of to-day, before then." The italics
are mine.

Yes, Charles Dickens very obligingly repeated this crucial speech
at a time when Jasper could and—I am convinced—did hear it. For
if "a cheerful sound of voices and laughter" could be "heard within"
the house by two men standing at the closed front door, I am confident that Jasper, with his ear close to the book-room window,
could have heard the statement made by Neville.

And mark how the young man goes on in his indictment of
Edwin Drood.

> "He goaded me, sir, beyond my power of endurance. I cannot say whether
> or no he meant it at first, but he did it. He certainly meant it at last. In short,
> sir," with an irrepressible outburst, "in the passion into which he lashed me,
> I would have cut him down if I could, and I tried to do it."

With an irrepressible outburst! Surely Neville's voice must have
been raised at this point, and surely a man standing outside the
window could have heard his words, uttered in loud tones. Indeed,
Dickens himself points up their volume not only by the phrase he
has used within the body of Neville's speech, but also by the contrasting adjective qualifying the Minor Canon's reply.

" 'You have clenched that hand again,' is Mr. Crisparkle's *quiet*
commentary." The italics are mine.

Note, too, that the Minor Canon, after showing Neville to his
bedroom and leaving him there, hears "another soft knock at the
outer door"—Jasper's knock—even "as he goes down-stairs." It
strikes me as highly significant that Dickens has, as it were, thus
gone out of his way to make it perfectly clear that sounds—whether
soft or loud—could readily be heard both from inside and outside
the Minor Canon's house. It may seem to the reader that I have
placed too much emphasis upon these little details. But as the
novelist himself wrote, in a letter to Wilkie Collins dated October 6,
1859: "I think the business of art is to lay all that ground carefully, not with the care that conceals itself—to show, by a backward
light, what everything has been working to,—but only to suggest,

until the fulfilment comes. These are the ways of Providence, of which ways all art is but a little imitation."

So I am confident that Jasper's eavesdropping, carried out in some manner similar to the one I have outlined, affords the only solution to the problem under discussion. Despite the mystification surrounding Neville Landless's first reference to "what is tigerish in their blood," and Jasper's subsequent use of the same figure of speech, final clarification of the situation comes with Neville's reiteration of the crucial remark—a reiteration wholly unnecessary unless Charles Dickens deemed it essential to the working of his plot. And finally, unless I am greatly mistaken, this simple yet rational solution will remove whatever feeling of bewilderment the reader may have at Jasper's almost verbatim repetition of young Landless's words.

Now that I have offered a solution to the problem, I consider it no more than fair to anticipate the natural reaction of some readers and to answer the following question: Why, in his brief conversation with the Minor Canon, did John Jasper find it necessary to employ the selfsame remarks so recently made by Neville Landless?

The answer to this question, I feel certain, depends upon the motive impelling the choirmaster to seek Mr. Crisparkle at so late an hour on so eventful a night. Elated with the outcome of the quarrel he had staged in his rooms between Neville Landless and his nephew, Edwin Drood, John Jasper has quite forgotten the humiliation he felt at the close of the piano scene. Not only does he experience a sense of triumph over his clever handling of the two young men, but he has also the assurance that he is beginning to pay back Miss Landless, the cause of his recent humiliation and a woman in whom he recognizes a dangerous adversary. What will she say when he has spread the news of the quarrel throughout Cloisterham and blackened her brother's reputation, as he has every intention of doing? Neville's carelessness in leaving his hat behind him provides Jasper with an excellent excuse for visiting the Minor Canon; yet it is not mere courtesy that takes him to Minor Canon

Corner, but rather his determination to impress upon Crisparkle the dangerous qualities inherent in young Landless's character. He means to avenge himself upon Miss Landless by a direct attack upon her brother, and to provide, at one and the same time, a likely suspect for the murder which he has long been plotting and which he will eventually commit.

Having overheard Neville utter the crucial speeches that form the basis of this discussion, he turns them to good account, and plays his part before Crisparkle with even greater relish. Always an opportunist, in the sense that he is quick to seize upon anything and everything that will further his own schemes, he stresses the murderous nature of Neville's attack upon Edwin by deliberately reiterating the "I would have cut him down" remark. Instantly aware of the obvious impression it makes upon the Minor Canon, he follows it up with the statement: "There is something of the tiger in his dark blood."

Then, careful not to overplay his hand, he leaves Crisparkle after voicing the prediction that the Minor Canon and Edwin may well be the objects of Neville's hostility. He is wholly satisfied with the over-all impression he has implanted in the Minor Canon's mind. Surely it is not too much to assert that at this point John Jasper is entertaining the comforting thought that, if his nephew Ned were to disappear, there would now be at hand not only a person *other than himself* who might logically be suspected of having caused that disappearance, but also an irreproachable witness to the suspected person's murderous nature. For John Jasper realizes, with almost diabolical intuition, that the repetition of Neville's remarks has somehow brought to Crisparkle's mind a deeper feeling of conviction than his own indictment of young Landless, *per se,* could possibly have established. He has merely reiterated what Neville himself had said to Crisparkle. In a very real sense, therefore, and because of John Jasper's clever emphasis on the ominous words proceeding from the young man's own mouth, Neville stands self-convicted as a potential murderer of Edwin Drood.

Jasper has achieved his purpose; he has even used the adjective "murderous" to qualify the scene which he himself staged between Neville and his nephew.

The dramatic events at the gatehouse occurred in chapter viii of the novel as we have it today, but it was chapter vii in the second number of the story as it was first set down by Dickens. This chapter should be followed by the one entitled "Mr. Durdles and Friend," which is chapter v of the novel in its current version. This confusing transposition of chapters is explained by a letter which Dickens wrote to Forster, which I quote from the famous biography:

"When I had written [Forster inserts: 22 December, 1869] and, as I thought, disposed of the first two Numbers of my story, Clowes informed me to my horror that they were, together, *twelve printed pages too short!!!* Consequently I had to transpose a chapter from number two to number one, and remodel number two altogether! This was the more unlucky, that it came upon me at the time when I was obliged to leave the book in order to get up the readings [Forster inserts: the additional twelve for which Sir Thomas Watson's consent had been obtained]; quite gone out of my mind since I left them off. However, I turned to it and got it done, and both numbers are now in type. Charles Collins has designed an excellent cover."

I shall follow Dickens's original order of chapters in my study of Jasper, for that sequence is more logical than the one forced upon the author by the discrepancy of pages which caused him nothing less than horror.

When Jasper is on his way home after his brief visit to Mr. Crisparkle, he comes upon Durdles, who is being stoned by the impish lad, Deputy. After it has been explained to him that the stoning is part of a ritual to urge Durdles homeward whenever he is abroad after ten o'clock, he offers to accompany the stonemason and suggests that he carry his dinner bundle. He is, of course, anxious to find out whether it still contains the key to the Sapsea monument. Durdles declines the offer, but points out various tombs in the churchyard near which they happen to be.

After shaking off Deputy, Jasper walks on with Durdles and brings up the cathedral crypt as a topic of conversation. This leads to the stonemason's curious existence, and to Jasper's proposal that Durdles allow him to go about with him and to visit some of the odd nooks in which he works.

" 'What I dwell upon most,' says Jasper, pursuing his subject of romantic interest, 'is the remarkable accuracy with which you would seem to find out where people are buried.—What is the matter? That bundle is in your way; let me hold it.' "

He relieves Durdles of the encumbrance, whereupon the stone-mason asks for his hammer.

"Clink, clink. And his hammer is handed him."

In this manner Dickens informs us that the key to the Sapsea monument is still in the bundle.

Durdles now gives Jasper a demonstration of his remarkable accuracy in locating buried persons. Tapping with his hammer, he explains his art of "solid in hollow; and inside solid, hollow again!" When Jasper voices his amazement, Durdles goes to even greater lengths in the display of his powers.

" 'Say that hammer of mine's a wall—my work,' " he announces. " 'Two; four; and two is six,' measuring on the pavement. 'Six foot inside that wall is Mrs. Sapsea.'

" 'Not really Mrs. Sapsea?'

" 'Say Mrs. Sapsea. Her wall's thicker, but say Mrs. Sapsea. Durdles taps that wall represented by that hammer, and says, after good sounding: "Something betwixt us!" Sure enough, *some rub-bish has been left in that same six-foot space* by Durdles's men!' " The italics are mine.

Here, in my opinion, is one of the most pertinent points made in this chapter. Some rubbish has been left in the six-foot space—rub-bish to which Jasper now plans to add something more gruesome: the remains of his nephew. Some writers have contended that the remarkable accuracy of Durdles in locating buried persons was to have been used by Dickens in the final discovery of the secret burial place of Edwin Drood. I hold that the foregoing scene is developed solely to make Jasper feel assured that Durdles would never be able to find any trace of Edwin's body if it were put inside the Sapsea monument. It would become part and parcel of the rubbish already there, and hence beyond suspicion. I maintain that, from this moment on, Jasper has solved his problem of where to dispose of Edwin's body.

Jasper and Durdles proceed on their way to the stonemason's home, and at no point in the remaining paragraphs of this chapter does Dickens tell us when Jasper gave up the dinner bundle. Indeed, there is no further mention whatsoever of the homely article so closely associated with Durdles. But note what Dickens does say with regard to Jasper.

"John Jasper returns by another way to his gatehouse, and entering softly *with his key,* finds his fire still burning." The italics are mine.

Now it strikes me as rather unlikely that Jasper would have locked his house door when he left earlier in the evening to return Neville's hat. He did not expect to be away for any length of time, and Edwin was in the gatehouse, as we are soon to learn. No, it is my firm conviction that Dickens is here being deliberately ambiguous, but that he is letting us infer that Jasper now has the key to the Sapsea monument. It will be simple enough for him to take an impression of it and to have a duplicate made at his leisure. But, it may be objected, how does he return the original key to the dinner bundle before Durdles is aware of its absence? Let me anticipate a bit, by jumping forward to the memorable chapter entitled "A Night with Durdles." Sapsea, now Mayor of Cloisterham, is chatting with the Dean, the Verger, and Jasper; in the course of their conversation the Dean remarks: "I hope, Mr. Mayor, you will use your study and knowledge of Durdles to the good purpose of exhorting him not to break our worthy and respected Choir-Master's neck"—a grim example of foreshadowing on Dickens's part when one considers the method of capital punishment employed in England.

Mr. Sapsea of course replies that he will answer for Mr. Jasper's neck. But how is it endangered?

"'Only by my making a moonlight expedition with Durdles among the tombs, vaults, towers, and ruins,' returns Jasper. 'You remember suggesting, when you brought us together, that, as a lover of the picturesque, it might be worth my while?'

"'*I* remember!' replies the auctioneer. And the solemn idiot really believes that he does remember."

Note what Jasper now says.

"'Profiting by your hint, I have had some day-rambles with the extraordinary old fellow, and we are to make a moonlight hole-and-corner exploration to-night.'"

Some day-rambles, indeed. It was on one of these—and it may well have been in the course of the first, which could easily have been made the day following Jasper's abstraction of the Sapsea key—that the Choirmaster returned the article in question to the dinner bundle. That is what I believe actually happened.

At any rate, to revert to the point at which I abandoned chronological order, Jasper has returned home. "He takes from a locked press a peculiar-looking pipe, which he fills—but not with tobacco—" and then goes up an inner staircase to contemplate his nephew as he lies sleeping. "Then, hushing his footsteps, he passes to his own room, lights his pipe, and delivers himself to the Spectres it invokes at midnight."

Well may he exult as he enters upon the opium-induced dreams in which he has already slain his nephew countless times! He now has a key to the Sapsea monument, and, better still, the assurance that that particular tomb will be the safest place of all in which to dispose of Edwin's body. The plan growing in that "horrible wonder apart" is progressing satisfactorily and without a flaw.

On the following morning, news of the quarrel between Edwin Drood and Neville Landless has reached Miss Twinkleton's establishment even before breakfast. Although Dickens does not tell us this in so many words, it is inferable that the report was spread by

Jasper. Certainly he told Mrs. Crisparkle of the affair, for she says to her son later in the story: "But for Mr. Jasper's well-bred consideration in coming up to me, next day, after service,—I believe I might never have heard of that disgraceful transaction." The China Shepherdess does not specify, but the incident to which she refers may well have taken place after the early morning service.

We are now introduced to Hiram Grewgious, the shrewd old lawyer who loved Rosa's mother and who has acted as the young girl's guardian ever since she became an orphan. He visits his ward at the Nuns' House and discharges various duties, chief among which is the satisfaction of his desire to learn whether Rosa wants to go through with her betrothal to Edwin. When he has completed this business, he goes to the cathedral, where he meets Jasper.

"Nothing is the matter?" Jasper asks him. "You have not been sent for?" The fact that he speaks "rather quickly" shows how disconcerted he is by the lawyer's presence in Cloisterham. Has anything occurred to upset his plan—now rapidly becoming an idée fixe?

Grewgious assures him that he has come of his own accord; that he found Rosa blooming; and that his purpose was to tell her "seriously, what a betrothal by deceased parents is."

" 'And what is it—according to your judgment?'

"Mr. Grewgious noticed the whiteness of the lips that asked the question, and put it down to the chilling account of the Cathedral." Again Jasper fears that something may be afoot to upset his plan.

The old lawyer informs Jasper that his sole intent was to tell Rosa that such a betrothal could not be binding if either party concerned had no real affection for the other, or inclination to carry it out.

"May I ask, had you any especial reason for telling her that?" is Jasper's query.

Mr. Grewgious retorts that he had only the especial reason of doing his duty, and that no disrespect to Edwin was implied.

" 'I will wager,' said Jasper, smiling—his lips were still so white that he was conscious of it, and bit and moistened them while speaking: 'I will wager that she hinted no wish to be released from Ned?' "

Grewgious assures him that he will win his wager, and eventually concludes: " '—she seems to have some little delicate instinct that all preliminary arrangements had best be made between Mr. Edwin Drood and herself, don't you see? She don't want us, don't you know?'

"Jasper touched himself on the breast, and said, somewhat indistinctly: 'You mean me.' " This is not a question, it should be noticed, but a statement of fact.

"Mr. Grewgious touched himself on the breast, and said: 'I mean us. Therefore, let them have their little discussions and councils together, when Mr. Edwin Drood comes back here at Christmas; and then you and I will step in, and put the final touches to the business.'

" 'So, you settled with her that you would come back at Christmas?' observed Jasper. 'I see!—I understand that at Christmas they will complete their preparations for May, and that their marriage will be put in final train by themselves, and that nothing will remain for us but to put ourselves in train also, and have everything ready for our formal release from our trusts, on Edwin's birthday.'

" 'That is my understanding,' assented Mr. Grewgious, as they shook hands to part. 'God bless them both!'

" 'God save them both!' cried Jasper."

His mind is made up; the plan must go through; Edwin must die.

" 'I said, bless them,' remarked the former, looking back over his shoulder.

" 'I said, save them,' returned the latter. 'Is there any difference?' " "

At this point I would direct the reader's attention to the fact that Grewgious, by what he has told Jasper, has set a relative time limit beyond which Edwin Drood may not remain alive. In this respect he has forced Jasper's hand, and is therefore, to a certain degree— albeit completely unaware of the situation and quite innocent,—responsible for the murder which is to come.

A few days later, Mr. Crisparkle has a talk with Helena and

Neville Landless, in the course of which he learns of the latter's love for Rosa. The Minor Canon exacts from Neville a pledge of absolute silence with respect to this love, also the promise that young Landless will make peace with Edwin, provided that Edwin make the first gesture toward the settling of their differences. To attain this end, Mr. Crisparkle hurries to the gatehouse, only to find Jasper asleep on a couch before the fire. "Long afterwards he had cause to remember how Jasper sprang from the couch in a delirious state between sleeping and waking, and crying out: 'What is the matter? Who did it?' "

Jasper has been dreaming his old dream; this time, it would seem that Edwin had already been murdered; the long-cherished plan has been carried out.

Jasper recovers himself, whereupon Mr. Crisparkle expresses his desire that peace may be established between Neville and Edwin. A very perplexed expression comes over Jasper's face, and he wants to know how such a result can be achieved. Mr. Crisparkle suggests that Jasper might induce Edwin to write a short note indicative of his willingness to shake hands.

"Jasper turned that perplexed face towards the fire. Mr. Crisparkle continuing to observe it, found it even more perplexing than before, inasmuch as it seemed to denote (which could hardly be) some close internal calculation."

But it can be, and does. Jasper's plan now involves Neville as Edwin's murderer-to-be; how can this aspect of things to come be made plausible if a reconciliation is effected between the two young men? Jasper is indeed calculating.

The Minor Canon tells Jasper that Neville has promised to maintain a friendly attitude toward Edwin, and that he himself will answer for young Landless.

Jasper agrees to do as the Minor Canon desires. He then shows Mr. Crisparkle two entries from his diary—a book later to assume even deeper significance—expressing his dread of what Neville may do to Edwin. Again he portrays Neville as a potential murderer.

Mr. Crisparkle advises Jasper to burn the diary, and departs when Jasper assures him that he will take care that his nephew shall "give way thoroughly."

On the third day after this interview, Jasper brings to the Minor Canon a letter from young Drood. After making honorable amends, Edwin writes to his uncle: "Ask Mr. Landless to dinner on Christmas eve (the better the day the better the deed) and let there be only we three, and let us shake hands all round there and then, and say no more about it."

" 'You expect Mr. Neville, then?' said Mr. Crisparkle.

" 'I count upon his coming,' said Mr. Jasper."

Indeed he does, since there is no doubt in my mind that he was entirely responsible for the request that Mr. Landless be asked to dinner on Christmas Eve, and that Edwin and he be the only others present. Again Jasper's hand has been forced, and the time schedule of his plan accelerated a little more. Now the good Minor Canon is unwittingly at fault. By his eagerness to establish peace between the young men, he has set an absolute time limit to Jasper's intent.

John Jasper—
Murderer

(PART TWO)

JASPER's next appearance is made in chapter xii, "A Night with Durdles," concerning which Dickens wrote in the notes jotted down for his eyes alone: "Lay the ground for the manner of the murder to come out at last." We learn at the beginning of this chapter that Mr. Sapsea not only has become Mayor of Cloisterham, but also has improved the acquaintance of Mr. Jasper. He has been received at the gatehouse; Jasper has sung to him and so tickled his vanity that the pompous Mayor considers him "sound, sir, at the core."

The chat between His Honor, the Dean, Mr. Tope the Verger, and Jasper—to which I have already alluded in my discussion of how Jasper came to possess a duplicate of the key to the Sapsea monument—is then related in detail, and so we come at last to the momentous moonlight expedition taken by Jasper and Durdles.

Jasper sits at his piano chanting choir music for two or three hours until the moon is about to rise. Then, equipped with "a goodly wicker-cased bottle," he goes to the stonemason's house.

As the two men start out for the cathedral, Durdles says: " 'Ware that there mound by the yard-gate, Mister Jarsper.'

" 'I see it. What is it?'

" 'Lime.'

"Mr. Jasper stops, and waits for him to come up, for he lags behind. 'What you call quick-lime?'

" 'Ay!' says Durdles; 'quick enough to eat your boots. With a little handy stirring, quick enough to eat your bones.' "

Jasper makes no comment, but we may be sure that Durdles's recipe is straightway registered in his mind, and that it becomes an integral part of his plan.

They hear the sound of a closing house door, and, standing behind a bit of old dwarf wall, see the Minor Canon accompanied by Neville coming out for a walk. As Jasper watches young Land-less, "a sense of destructive power" is expressed in his face. His plan is well-nigh perfected, and here is the very man who is to bear the guilt of its fulfillment! Mr. Crisparkle is evidently telling Neville about Edwin's letter to Jasper, for Neville says: "You may be certain of me, sir." When they move on out of sight, Jasper "turns to Durdles, and bursts into a fit of laughter." Assured that his chosen scapegoat will be at the select dinner on Christmas Eve, he cannot refrain from open exultation.

Dickens now makes such a point of describing the "certain awful hush" which pervades the cathedral, the cloisters, and the church-yard, and so emphasizes the fact that the good citizens of Cloister-ham shun these precincts, that the veriest novice can perceive that a man may go about some strange, unusual business there and yet escape observation.

The two explorers go down to the crypt, locking themselves in. As they wander up and down, Durdles discourses of the " 'old uns' he yet counts on disinterring." Jasper's wicker bottle circulates freely, so far as the stonemason is concerned—but "Mr. Jasper only rinses his mouth once, and casts forth the rinsing." This can only mean that Jasper has drugged the contents of the bottle.

Before they ascend the great tower, Durdles pauses for breath. He tells Jasper how he was set upon by town boys a year ago, and turned in to the cathedral. He fell asleep, but was awakened by the ghost of a cry. This was followed by the ghost of a dog's howl. "That was *my* last Christmas Eve," he concludes.

" 'What do you mean?' is the very abrupt, and, one might say, fierce retort."

Jasper's mind is so intent upon his plan to murder his nephew that Durdles's emphasis of the possessive adjective leads him to wonder whether Durdles has any suspicion of what occupies that "horrible wonder apart"; whether he has an inkling that the Christmas Eve now approaching is to be Edwin's last.

They go up the winding stairway of the tower and finally look down upon Cloisterham. It is worth noting that Jasper contemplates not only the moonlight view of the panorama spread before him, but "especially that stillest part of it which the Cathedral overshadows"—the churchyard.

The drugged liquor has its effect: Durdles becomes drowsy. They descend into the crypt, where Durdles "appeals to his companion for forty winks of a second each.

" 'If you will have it so, or must have it so,' replies Jasper, 'I'll not leave you here. Take them, while I walk to and fro.'

"Durdles is asleep at once.—He dreams that the footsteps die away into distance of time and of space, and that something touches him, and that something falls from his hand." Jasper has come up to him softly and removed from his grasp the key to the crypt, which Durdles still holds after locking the iron gate. As he does so, the key falls to the pavement. "Then something clinks and gropes about, and he dreams that he is alone for so long a time, that the lanes of light take new directions as the moon advances in her course."

This is indeed true, for Jasper, after recovering the key of the crypt from where it has fallen, lets himself out and goes about his sinister business. It takes him first to Durdles's yard, which overlooks the churchyard, as Mr. Percy Carden has proved by his study of the original manuscript. There he finds a wheelbarrow and loads it with quicklime. It is reasonably inferable that he might find such a means of conveyance, and a spade, at the stonemason's. Having his duplicate key to the Sapsea monument with him, he then proceeds to open the tomb and add to the rubbish already there enough lime to consume a body. The moon affords him sufficient light for his grim labors. By the time he has finished them, returned the implements he has borrowed, brushed off his clothes, and rejoined Durdles, who finally rouses from his sleep, it is two o'clock.

The key to the crypt door is now lying close to Durdles.

It should be noted that just before the two men ascended the tower, Jasper took the stonemason's dinner bundle. Now, as they are about to leave the cathedral, Durdles says: " 'Let me get my bundle right, Mister Jarsper, and I'm with you.'

"As he ties it afresh, he is once more conscious that he is very narrowly observed."

Now I do not believe that Jasper waited until this eventful night to avail himself of the key to the Sapsea monument. He could not depend upon the original, which was in Durdles's keeping; the very nature of his plan would demand that he have a duplicate of his own. He would certainly need one for further use, and I have already indicated how he obtained it. But I do believe that he wanted to find out whether Durdles still had the original, or whether it had been returned to Mr. Sapsea. Jasper is playing a desperate game, in which he cannot afford to overlook even so slight a detail as this. I likewise believe that Dickens wanted the reader to assume that Jasper took the key to the Sapsea monument from the dinner bundle on this particular night; the reader would then be all the more at sea in his endeavor to figure out how Jasper could again unlock the tomb on the night of Edwin's murder. I am morally certain that Jasper had a duplicate key, obtained in the way I have demonstrated, and that he kept it in his locked press with his opium pipe.

As the two men separate to go their respective ways homeward, Deputy yelps out his "Widdy widdy wen!" jargon, and pelts Durdles with stones.

" 'What! Is that baby-devil on the watch there!' cries Jasper in a fury: so quickly roused, and so violent, that he seems an older devil himself. 'I shall shed the blood of that impish wretch! I know I shall do it!' "

He is desperately afraid that Deputy has seen him at work in Durdles's yard or near the Sapsea monument—as probably he has, in view of the note Dickens wrote for his own use: "Keep the boy suspended." Jasper rushes at Deputy and takes him by the throat, and it is not until the imp declares that he had just come out for his health when he saw the two men emerge from the cathedral that Jasper is somewhat appeased. But, even so, "he goes to his gatehouse, brooding."

A few days later, Jasper, standing under the elm trees by the cathedral, sees Edwin and Rosa kiss each other good-bye. To him, this kiss is a fervent expression of the love existing between his nephew and the young woman for whom he himself entertains a lustful passion. He does not know that Edwin and Rosa have agreed to break off their engagement: Edwin, because he has been sobered by an interview he has had with old Grewgious; Rosa, because she has long realized that she can love Edwin only as a brother. He does not know that Edwin carries with him a ring of diamonds and rubies, once the property of Rosa's mother, which Grewgious has given to young Drood with the solemn injunction that it is to be brought back to him if, for any reason whatsoever, Edwin does not place it upon Rosa's finger as a token of their mutual desire to go through with their marriage. Only three persons know that Edwin has this ring: Grewgious; Bazzard, the old lawyer's clerk; and Edwin himself.

"He saw us, as we took leave of each other," Edwin says to Rosa. "Poor fellow! he little thinks we have parted. This will be a blow to him, I am much afraid!"

They have previously agreed that Jasper must be told of their decision, and Rosa has suggested that the information be given him by her guardian, Grewgious.

Rosa hurries on, because she cannot bear to be near Jasper, until she and Edwin are at the door of the Nuns' House. "Before going in, she gave him one last, wide, wondering look, as if she would have asked him with imploring emphasis: 'O! don't you understand?'"

Because she has proposed that Grewgious break the news of their agreement to separate, thus sealing Edwin's lips, and because she has never spoken to young Drood of the passion which, as she realizes only too well, Jasper feels for her, Rosa, too, in all her innocence, is partly responsible for the fate awaiting her erstwhile fiancé. That parting kiss, overseen by Jasper, has irrevocably sealed his nephew's doom.

And now it is Christmas Eve in Cloisterham—the eve of that Holy Birthday of which Dickens had so often extolled the sacred and festive spirit in his Christmas books and stories. By some strange revulsion of feeling he now casts aside his "Carol" philosophy to choose December 25th as the day for Edwin Drood's murder.

Neville Landless spends most of the day before Christmas in preparation for a walking tour; he cannot endure the thought of being a witness to Rosa's happiness at this joyous time. He finally goes to the dinner at the gatehouse with a strange presentiment of something fearful to come.

Edwin Drood passes a lonely day, but makes one visit which is of extreme importance. Finding that his watch has stopped, he calls at the jeweler's to have it wound and set. The jeweler seeks to interest him in some of his stock, but "Edwin tells the tempter that he wears no jewellery but his watch and chain, which were his father's; and his shirt-pin."

Mark how Dickens emphasizes the heirlooms and the pin.

" 'That I was aware of,' is the jeweller's reply, 'for Mr. Jasper dropped in for a watch-glass the other day, and, in fact, I showed these articles to him, remarking that if he *should* wish to make a present to a gentleman relative, on any particular occasion—But he said with a smile that he had an inventory in his mind of all the jewellery his gentleman relative ever wore; namely, his watch and chain, and his shirt-pin.' "

It would appear that Jasper broke his watch glass on the night when he made the moonlight expedition with Durdles.

"Twenty minutes past two, Mr. Drood, I set your watch at," says the jeweler. "Let me recommend you not to let it run down, sir."

Edwin goes out and later meets the Opium Woman, who has come to Cloisterham "looking for a needle in a haystack," meaning Jasper. After Edwin gives her some money, she tells him that "Ned" is a threatened name, a dangerous name to bear. Young Drood is somewhat dismayed as he goes to the dinner; he "resolves—to say nothing of this tonight, but to mention it to Jack (who alone calls him Ned), as an odd coincidence, to-morrow."

John Jasper spends an agreeable and cheerful day. With a grim *double entendre,* of which he was sometimes capable, Dickens has him tell the shopkeepers that "his nephew will not be with him long." He informs Mr. Sapsea of the dinner he plans to give at the gatehouse, whereupon His Honor speaks in an unfriendly manner of Neville. It is clear that Jasper has voiced his fears with respect to young Landless in His Honor's presence.

Moved by a kind of sardonic humor, Dickens remarks that Jasper is in beautiful voice on this day, but that "the mere mechanism of his throat is a little tender, for he wears—a large black scarf of strong close-woven silk, slung loosely round his neck." Meeting Mr. Crisparkle, he tells him that he means to burn his diary at the end of the year. He then makes for the gatehouse, but before he goes up to his rooms, he pauses to "pull off that great black scarf, and hang it in a loop upon his arm. For that brief time, his face is knitted and stern."

It is probably this same black scarf, more than anything else, which led Mr. Howard Duffield to write "John Jasper—Strangler," an essay extremely ingenious in its presentation of the theory that Jasper belonged to a secret band of Thugs, and that by murdering his nephew he was carrying out a ritual killing in the service of Kali, Goddess of Destruction. I do not accept this theory, for the following reasons.

First of all, Jasper is introduced to us as a man of some six-and-twenty; he is therefore comparatively young. When one considers all that he has accomplished, his very age militates against the possibility of his being a Thug. He must have received his schooling in

England; he certainly talks like an educated man, and he uses English idiom. He must also have spent some time taking piano and voice lessons in order to occupy the position he actually holds. He is choirmaster of Cloisterham Cathedral, and a teacher of some ability. I cannot conceive how he had time to serve apprenticeship in the vast brotherhood of Thugs while preparing himself for such a position as the one in which we find him. And, were he a true Thug, I fail to comprehend how he could associate himself, as he does, with the Anglican Catholic Church.

But Mr. Duffield states that Jasper's appearance suggests his Oriental origin. Is this not a somewhat far-fetched conclusion, reached merely because Jasper is dark and has "thick, lustrous, well-arranged black hair and whiskers"? Now Jasper's sister was Edwin's mother, yet Mr. Duffield does not suggest that her son shows any indications of being an Oriental. Perhaps Mr. Duffield was influenced by the fact that Jasper smokes opium. So did Thomas De Quincey, yet I know of no suggestion that he was of Oriental origin.

Some of Mr. Duffield's statements are so open to argument that his whole theory, arresting though it is, leaves me unconvinced. He says of Jasper, for example: "Incidentally, he is shown to be familiar with the languages of the East, for, when he listens to the mutterings of the opium-drenched Chinaman and the Lascar, he recognizes them as 'unintelligible gibberish.'" Because a man exclaims "Unintelligible!" when he hears the incoherent ramblings of a Chinaman or a Lascar, I do not see how it is proved that he can himself speak Chinese or an East Indian dialect. Furthermore, at no place in the first chapter does Dickens use the word "gibberish." As a matter of fact, when Jasper addresses the Chinaman, he asks: "What do you say?" If he were familiar with the language, why did he not question him in Chinese?

Again, Mr. Duffield says: "One of the most prominent characters has pinned upon him the grotesque title of 'Tartar,' a name as redolent of the East as a whiff of hashish." Now I should hardly call Tartar "one of the most prominent characters" in the novel. We

cannot tell how much Dickens may have planned to develop him
later, but of the twenty-three chapters constituting the fragment as
we have it, he actually appears in only three. As to his title, I can
myself suggest a way in which Dickens might have created it which
is as English as roast beef. First Lieutenant Tartar, late of the Royal
Navy? "Tar" is a common synonym for "sailor," short for "jack-
tar." Double the common synonym and you have "Tartar," a name
which has a whiff of the sea.

One more quotation from Mr. Duffield's article, and I have done.
"The literary atmosphere in which *The Mystery of Edwin Drood*
was cradled was dense with a kind of germ for which Dickens's
imagination was genial soil, and which would inevitably fructify
into a story essentially akin to *The Moonstone*—which novel, it is
worth noting, contributed, almost verbatim, one crucial paragraph
to the Drood narrative."

I have ransacked Wilkie Collins's great novel for the paragraph
in question. I offer my sincere apologies to Mr. Duffield if I am
wrong, but I am forced to the conclusion that he must have meant
the following one:

"Dr. Abel informed me," says Mr. Combe, "of an Irish porter to
a warehouse, who forgot, when sober, what he had done when
drunk; but, being drunk, again recollected the transactions of his
former state of intoxication. On one occasion, being drunk, he had
lost a parcel of some value, and in his sober moments could give no
account of it. Next time he was intoxicated he recollected that he
had left a parcel at a certain house, and there being no address on
it, it had remained there safely, and was got on his calling for it."

Of course, the foregoing paragraph immediately suggests the one
from *The Mystery of Edwin Drood* which I quote below; but I
fail to see how Mr. Duffield is justified in his use of the phrase
"almost verbatim."

"As, in some cases of drunkenness, and in others of animal magnetism, there are two states of consciousness which never clash, but
each of which pursues its separate course as though it were continu-

ous instead of broken (thus, if I hide my watch when I am drunk, I must be drunk again before I can remember where), so Miss Twinkleton has two distinct and separate phases of being."

It is true that Dickens had read *Confessions of a Thug,* by Captain Meadows Taylor, who was a contributor to Dickens's magazine. The book is a long-winded, picaresque tale—somewhat reminiscent of *The Arabian Nights,*—based on Taylor's personal experiences in India in the service of H.H. the Nizam. It contains references to opium, and one allusion to quicklime. It is perhaps worth mentioning that Taylor uses quotations from *Macbeth* and that there are three references to the same tragedy in *The Mystery of Edwin Drood.* Dickens may well have taken from Taylor's story some of the Thug methods—notably, murder by strangulation,—but I am still by no means convinced that John Jasper was an Oriental, or a member of a band of Thugs.

As occurred a few days before the murder of Montague Tigg by Jonas Chuzzlewit, a storm of unprecedented fury rages on the eve of the disappearance of Edwin Drood. "But early in the morning, when there is barely enough light in the east to dim the stars, it begins to lull."

A group of idlers watching some workmen occupied by an examination of damage done to the cathedral tower by the tempest is shoved aside by Mr. Jasper, who calls loudly to Mr. Crisparkle, "at an open window.

" 'Where is my nephew?'

" 'He has not been here. Is he not with you?'

" 'No. He went down to the river last night, with Mr. Neville, to look at the storm, and has not been back. Call Mr. Neville!' "

Jasper's solicitude for the whereabouts of his "dear Ned" comes a trifle late, but his dramatic outburst has its desired effect. "There is no more looking up at the tower, now."

Neville is sought and apprehended soon after leaving an inn eight miles distant from Cloisterham. Since he does not submit to capture without a struggle, his clothing and walking stick become bloodstained. No sooner is he brought before Mr. Crisparkle and Jasper than the latter begins to address him as the man responsible for Edwin's disappearance. Where is his nephew, Jasper wants to know.

"I ask you because you were the last person in his company, and he is not to be found."

Neville, because of his complete innocence, is utterly bewildered by the situation. He admits that he left the gatehouse at midnight in company with Edwin, that they went to the river to see the action of the wind there, and that they remained for some ten minutes. They then walked to Mr. Crisparkle's, where young Drood took leave of Neville and said he was going back to his uncle's.

Jasper immediately draws attention to the bloodstains on Neville's clothing and stick. Despite the wholly plausible explanation for their presence on these articles, Neville is brought before Mr. Sapsea.

My conclusions derived from the foregoing happenings are that Jasper murdered Edwin Drood between 12:30 and 1:00 o'clock on Christmas morning, and that the slaying took place in Jasper's rooms at the gatehouse. Only after the violence of the storm had abated, "early in the morning," when there was "barely enough light in the east to dim the stars," could he have removed the body to the Sapsea tomb.

Once in the presence of His Honor, Jasper capitalizes on the ascendancy he has gained over Sapsea. He insinuates to such good purpose that Neville is the guilty man that Sapsea is about to consign young Landless to jail, when Mr. Crisparkle undertakes to be responsible for him and for his appearance "whenever demanded." Again by insinuation, Jasper suggests "that particulars of the disappearance should be sent to all outlying places and to London, and that placards and advertisements should be widely circulated imploring Edwin Drood, if for any unknown reason he had withdrawn himself from his uncle's home and society, to take pity on that loving kinsman's sore bereavement and distress, and somehow inform him that he was yet alive." All this is done.

During the next two days, an intensive search for Edwin's body is made on the river and along its banks. Jasper works with the searchers, and on the evening of the second day returns home to find Mr. Grewgious waiting for him. Rosa has sent for the old lawyer, and in one of the novel's most dramatic passages Grewgious informs Jasper that Rosa and Edwin had amicably broken off their engagement.

This devastating news is too much for Jasper to bear; with a terrible shriek, he faints dead away. Blinded by his passion for Rosa, he has killed his nephew, whom he once loved, because of a situation which was nonexistent when the murder was done. Grewgious, though he says nothing, now recognizes him for the murderer that he is.

When he recovers consciousness, Jasper strives desperately to make the best of a most difficult situation. At any cost, he must clear himself of all suspicion. He therefore suggests that Edwin may have fled of his own free will rather than face the awkwardness of his position, resulting from the termination of his long-standing engagement with Rosa. Dickens's private notes refer to this stand as "Jasper's artful use of the communication on his recovery."

He continues to urge such a possibility by stating in the presence of Mr. Crisparkle, who has joined them, that "there was no quarrel or difference between the two young men at their last meeting"—which is undoubtedly the truth. He now exonerates Neville of all guilt, playing the hypocrite not only because he realizes the old lawyer's shrewdness, but because he fears Helena Landless. He believes that his present pose will make his own position stronger.

But now Mr. Crisparkle looses another thunderbolt on Jasper's head. In his desire to be equally honest with Grewgious, the Minor Canon informs the old lawyer of his certainty that Neville will be cleared of all suspicion despite his hot temper, even despite the fact that he declared himself to be in love with Rosa.

Though the Minor Canon's revelation has "turned him paler," Jasper maintains his stand. He will cling to his hope that Edwin has disappeared voluntarily unless some trace of him is found "leading to the dreadful inference that he had been done away with."

Since Jasper, in his now almost maddened state of mind, has created for himself a loophole whereby he may continue to pursue Neville as Edwin's murderer, such a trace is soon forthcoming. Early on the morning of the next day, Mr. Crisparkle finds on Cloisterham Weir a chain and a gold watch, with the initials "E. D." engraved on its back. When he dives repeatedly with the expectation of recovering Edwin's body, he finally brings up Edwin's shirt pin.

That Jasper planted these articles on the weir is the only possible inference to be drawn from the evidence brought out when Neville is taken once again before Mayor Sapsea. Dickens does not make His Honor speak in person—which is a pity,—but merely summarizes his findings. "The watch found at the Weir was challenged by the jeweller as one he had wound and set for Edwin Drood, at twenty minutes past two on that same afternoon [of the day before Christmas]; and it had run down, before being cast into the water; and it was the jeweller's positive opinion that it had never been rewound."

Now, the watch had not been cast into the water; it was caught by its chain among the interstices of the timbers forming the weir. And Jasper, with the knowledge of his crime fresh in mind, had never thought of winding the watch after he had removed it from Edwin's dead body. He had of course realized that non-corrosive metals must not accompany the corpse to its bier of quicklime.

Sapsea's findings continue. "If he had been murdered, and *so artfully disfigured* [the italics are mine], or concealed, or both, as that the murderer hoped identification to be impossible, except from something that he wore, assuredly the murderer would seek to remove from the body the most lasting, the best known, and the most easily recognizable, things upon it. Those things would be the watch and shirt-pin."

"So artfully disfigured"! Can anyone doubt that Jasper has been at work on His Honor, or that this insinuation came from him? What reason could Sapsea have to believe that Edwin had been disfigured, even though murdered, and his jewelry removed to prevent identification? The watch and pin might more logically have been taken because they were valuables. They might well have been thrown on the weir by a panic-stricken killer in his flight. And why should His Honor employ the phrase "the most lasting"? But Jasper, having used quicklime to ensure the destruction of his nephew's body—as he did,—knows that the remains will be disfigured; and that noncorrosive objects—the most lasting—must not be left on the corpse; his knowledge of these facts breaks through His Honor's circumlocutions. My contention is that he thus overreaches himself and gives himself away.

Neville is detained and redetained, while the search for Edwin Drood goes on. At last young Landless is set free, because there is no *corpus delicti*. But he has to leave Cloisterham under a cloud of suspicion; a social pariah, he goes to London, where he is befriended by Mr. Crisparkle and Grewgious.

John Jasper, a day or two later, shows Mr. Crisparkle a page from his diary worth analyzing. It begins: "My dear boy is murdered." This is an assertion, and well may Jasper make it. "The discovery of the watch and shirt-pin convinces me that he was murdered that night, and that his jewellery was taken from him to prevent identification by its means." Here again, Jasper reveals his own guilt. Suppose Edwin has been murdered by a man who dashed his brains out with a club—or who strangled him—and took the jewelry from him to prevent identification by its means. Such a murderer would realize that the body could still be identified by the facial features, by its clothing, or by any distinguishing marks which might exist. He would be mad merely to remove the watch and shirt pin in the hope of preventing identification. But Jasper, who has concealed his nephew's body in the Sapsea tomb, where he covered it with quicklime, knows full well that the removal of the jewelry will prevent identification of the body *by its means*. And I maintain that here again Jasper betrays himself as Edwin's murderer.

The page continues: "All the delusive hopes I had founded on his separation from his betrothed wife, I give to the winds. They perish before this fatal discovery. I now swear, and record the oath on this page, That I nevermore will discuss this mystery with any human creature until I hold the clue to it in my hand." He realizes that he has already talked too much for his own good—to Hiram Grewgious. "That I never will relax in my secrecy or in my search. That I will fasten the crime of the murder of my dear dead boy upon the murderer." He is thinking of Neville Landless, destined to be the next victim of that "horrible wonder apart." "And, That I devote myself to his destruction."

Here I must direct attention to the letter Dickens wrote to John Forster on Friday, August 6, 1869: "I laid aside the fancy I told you of, and have a very curious and new idea for my new story. Not a communicable idea (or the interest of the book would be gone), but a very strong one, though difficult to work."

What was this "very curious and new idea"? I believe it may be summed up in a few sentences. A man—John Jasper—plans to commit a perfect murder because he is driven to it by one of the oldest and most powerful motives: passion for a woman. As I have already shown, perfectly innocent persons—Grewgious, Mr. Crisparkle, and Rosa—are indirectly responsible for the fact that the murder is done at a certain time. The murder, successfully committed if we consider the period with its infantile knowledge of scientific methods of criminal investigation, later proves to have been needless. Then a perfectly innocent person—Minor Canon Crisparkle—unwittingly restores the *status quo,* with Neville Landless in the position of Edwin Drood. The murderer has to begin all over again. So he devotes himself to the destruction of—*himself,* as Mr. Montagu Saunders perceived; for all his subsequent plotting to destroy his victim will merely make certain his own guilt. The innocent contributors to the first crime will, in varying ways, help to track down the murderer, thus avenging a death for which they themselves have been partly to blame. Instead of attacking social evils in his last novel, Dickens will have society itself coming down on a lone, offending member. The ring of diamonds and rubies will be the only existing clue to Edwin's identity and place of burial. John Jasper knows absolutely nothing about this ring—as yet. Certainly this summary embodies an idea which might be termed "curious and new," and in view of Dickens's physical and mental condition when he began to develop it, "difficult to work."

Six months after the disappearance of Edwin Drood, we find Jasper in London, going about his dark business with the intent of putting the blame for the murder of his nephew squarely on Neville's shoulders. He is spying upon him, and is in turn spied upon by old Hiram Grewgious, who has taken an interest in Neville.

About this same time, he calls upon Rosa when she is alone at the Nuns' House. School has just closed for the year, and Helena Landless has gone to London to be with her brother. Rosa has never seen Jasper "since the fatal night, except when she was questioned before the Mayor." But now, by the sun dial in the garden, hypocritically dressed in mourning, he is waiting to speak to her. "The old horrible feeling of being compelled by him, asserts its hold upon her."

Jasper tells her that he has been waiting to be summoned back as her "faithful music-master." When she informs him that she has left off that study, he insists that it has been but discontinued, and upbraids her for not having loved Edwin in the right way. When she insists that she will study no more with him, and that she does not care to be subjected to further questioning, he tells her that he will confess—

" 'I do not wish to hear you, sir,' cries Rosa, rising."

He threatens that she must listen to him, or she will do more harm to others than she can ever set right.

" 'Sit down, and there will be no mighty wonder in your music-master's leaning idly against a pedestal and speaking with you, remembering all that has happened, and our shares in it.' "

He is accusing her of having been responsible for Edwin's disappearance because she never revealed to her fiancé the love she knew his uncle bore her. And his use of "our" is an admission that he, too, is culpable.

He now lays bare to her his mad passion, intensifying it by the most extravagant terms. "—In the distasteful work of the day, in the wakeful misery of the night, girded by sordid realities, or wandering through Paradises and Hells of visions into which I rushed, carrying your image in my arms, I loved you madly!"

With great indignation, Rosa rebukes him, accusing him of being false to his nephew and of causing her such fear that she dared not open Edwin's eyes.

"How beautiful you are!" is his rejoinder. "You are more beautiful in anger than repose. I don't ask you for your love; give me yourself and your hatred; give me yourself and that pretty rage; give me yourself and that enchanting scorn; it will be enough for me."

The barriers are down at last; the man reveals to her in all its nakedness the lust that burns within him.

Forcing her to remain despite her tears, he tells her that, had the ties between him and his nephew been less strong, he might even have swept Edwin from his side when she favored him. Now he has heard that Neville Landless loves her, and that is an inexpiable offense in his eyes. He has devoted himself to the destruction of Edwin's murderer and will work in silence until he holds the clue with which he may entangle that murderer as in a net.

"I have since worked patiently to wind and wind it round him; and it is slowly winding as I speak."

Rosa retorts that his belief in Mr. Landless's criminality is evil.

"Circumstances may accumulate so strongly *even against an innocent man,* that directed, sharpened, and pointed, they may slay him. One wanting link discovered by perseverance against a guilty man proves his guilt, however slight its evidence before, and he dies. Young Landless stands in deadly peril either way."

Since he is seeking to terrify Rosa, the second sentence of his speech is meant to impress her even more strongly than the first. He may yet destroy Neville, even though innocent, if he can convince Sapsea of his guilt; but if he can find some means to prove it—some tangible evidence that will damn him,—there is not the faintest ray of hope for Landless! How little does he realize that he foretells his own fate; how little does he dream that the ring of diamonds and rubies will be the "one wanting link" he craves, the link which will brand him, not young Landless, a murderer to all the world!

Rosa disclaims any affection for Neville, protesting that he has never addressed himself to her in any way.

Jasper now offers her a bribe typical of his villainy. If she will accept his love, he will renounce his pursuit of Neville; her dear friend Helena will preserve her peace of mind, her good name, and the shadow of the gallows will be removed from her. He even casts away his fidelity to Edwin after death; the love Neville bears Rosa; his labors of six months in the cause of "just" vengeance.

"There is my past and my present wasted life. There is the desolation of my heart and soul. There is my peace; there is my despair. Stamp them into the dust; so that you take me, were it even mortally hating me!"

Thus he concludes. Rosa is so stunned and terrified that she moves swiftly away from him.

"Not a word of this to any one," he warns her, "or it will bring down the blow, as certainly as night follows day."

With one last mad declaration of his passion, in which he swears that she will never be rid of him, that he will pursue her even to death, he leaves her.

Rosa faints as she goes upstairs to her room. Later, when she has recovered, she flees to London to her old guardian, Grewgious. Earlier, I have shown how her plight—as well as that of Neville and his sister—so move the old lawyer that he takes an active part in a campaign to track down Jasper and prove him the murderer of his nephew. To do so, he goes to Cloisterham disguised as Dick Datch-ery, leaving Rosa in the care of Miss Twinkleton, who comes to London to be with his ward. Rosa's horrible ordeal with Jasper is soon dispelled from her mind by her interest in Neville's friend, Lieutenant Tartar, who returns that interest in full measure.

And so the forces of society begin to range themselves against the lone offender, for such has Jasper become. "Impassive, moody, solitary, resolute, so concentrated on one idea, and on its attendant fixed purpose, that he would share it with no fellow creature, he lived apart from human life." "The spirit of the man was in moral accordance or interchange with nothing around him."

"Again, when the wicked man turneth away from his wickedness that he hath committed, and doeth that which is lawful and right, he shall save his soul alive." That is the Law and the Prophet, but Jasper has not heeded them. And so he pursues his way to inevitable destruction.

The verse from Ezekiel moves me to wonder how far Dickens may have identified himself with the murderer whose mind—that "horrible wonder apart"—he was studying. Is it not conceivable that in his last novel Dickens was taking himself to task for having flouted the moral code of his day, for having separated from his wife and broken up his home because he—like John Jasper—became in-fatuated with a lovely young woman? If such a conception is im-possible, why did Dickens quote the verse in the abbreviated form which appears in the opening chapter? Did he set it down only in part because of his realization that it applied to him? It is a verse resplendent with hope and with the promise of forgiveness. Neither that hope nor that promise of forgiveness could apply to Jasper, in whose tortured soul there was no spark of contrition. But the words of the prophet must have had meaning for the man who could write—among the last he was ever to set down on paper—the following lines: "Changes of glorious light from moving boughs, songs of birds, scents from gardens, woods, and fields—or, rather, from the one great garden of the whole cultivated island in its yielding time—penetrate into the Cathedral, subdue its earthy odour, and preach the Resurrection and the Life."

Almost our last glimpse of John Jasper finds him in London on a hot, dusty evening, hurrying to the opium den where we first met him. His need for the drug ended, for a time, with Edwin's death. Now he craves it again because Rosa has fled, because he plans to destroy Neville. The old Opium Woman welcomes him like a long-lost stranger, but she seems more interested in plying him with questions than in serving his needs; she has seen the "placards and advertisements" which appeared in London after his nephew disappeared. However, he is soon under the influence of the drug—which does not taste the same, and now appears to have a slower reaction upon him. All of which leads me to believe that the old Opium Woman has weakened her mixture, for a purpose of her own.

"Suppose you had something in your mind; something you were going to do," Jasper says to her.

"Yes, deary; something I was going to do?"

"Should you do it in your fancy, when you were lying here doing this?"

"Over and over again."

He is thinking of Neville Landless, and of the destruction he must bring upon him.

"Just like me!" he goes on. "I did it over and over again. I have done it hundreds of thousands of times in this room."

Now his opium-drugged thoughts have reverted to Edwin.

"It's to be hoped it was pleasant to do, deary."

"It *was* pleasant to do!—It was a journey, a difficult and danger-out journey.—A hazardous and perilous journey, over abysses where a slip would be destruction. Look down, look down! You see what lies at the bottom there?"

He fancies himself on the cathedral tower, pointing to the Sapsea tomb far below in the churchyard.

"I did it so often, and through such vast expanses of time, that when it was really done, it seemed not worth the doing, it was done so soon."

This is a virtual confession to the murder of Edwin Drood.

"Hark!" He hears the cathedral bells sounding the half hour.

"Time and place are both at hand." Half an hour after midnight on Christmas morning—and he and Edwin are together in the gate-house.

"No struggle, no consciousness of peril, no entreaty—and yet I never saw *that* before."

He strangled Edwin from behind, with his great black scarf. But in his dreams of the past he could not visualize the actual appearance of a dead body. Now he knows what it looks like.

"Look at it! Look what a poor, mean, miserable thing it is! *That* must be real. It's over."

It *is* real—no figment of his hallucinations now.

He lapses into oblivion, while the Opium Woman congratulates herself that she may have learned the secret of how to make him talk.

When he departs at last, the old hag follows him, and having found out that he intends to return to Cloisterham at six that same evening, goes to the cathedral city before him. There she awaits his arrival, then pursues him to the gatehouse, where she meets Datch-ery. In the course of their conversation, Datchery learns that she met and talked with Edwin on that last Christmas Eve. The man who is tracking Jasper down tells the woman she may see the choirmaster in the cathedral the very next morning. Then he seeks Deputy, with whom he has struck up an acquaintance, to give him the task of searching out the creature's address.

The next day dawns, and from a point of vantage in the cathedral Datchery sees the Opium Woman shake her fist at Mr. Jasper, hug herself in her lean arms, and then shake both fists at the choirmaster.

That is our last glimpse of John Jasper; for death stilled forever the hand of the man who was weaving the threads of his destiny into their final pattern. Charles Dickens was stricken on the very day when he was completing the chapter I have just been discussing. A few deductions based on my prolonged investigation of the novel as he left it may serve to bring this study to a close.

Hiram Grewgious, alias Dick Datchery, knows now why Edwin Drood never returned the ring of diamonds and rubies: he was prevented from doing so because he died in Cloisterham, murdered by his uncle. Grewgious realizes also that the Opium Woman is going to blackmail Jasper, for she, too, suspects him of the murder of his nephew. If he were to learn, through her, of the presence of the ring on Edwin's person, he would reveal the place where the body lay buried in an attempt to retrieve the evidence that damns him. Prior to this dénouement, however, Helena Landless, dressed in her brother's clothes and playing his part, will confront Jasper and will try to make him incriminate himself through the exercise of her hypnotic power. This attempt will, I feel certain, be unsuccessful.

When Jasper is finally surprised at the Sapsea tomb, he will try to escape by way of the cathedral tower, which he will ascend to commit suicide. Neville Landless will be mortally wounded in pursuit of him, and will die after learning that his innocence has been established. Tartar and Mr. Crisparkle will take Jasper alive. Then will come his confession from the death cell, given as though he were speaking of some other person. And indeed he will be doing just that, for the "horrible wonder apart" will now be so warped and twisted by all its owner has been through that it will no longer belong to the man known in Cloisterham as John Jasper.

He who was respected as lay precentor and choirmaster will be hanged by the neck until dead—which is just another form of strangulation. He will be dumped into an unmarked grave, where his body will be covered with quicklime. Justice, both man-made and poetic, will have been done, for so he treated his nephew, whom he once loved. The wheel will have come full circle.

Out of the depths of his despair and shame, Oscar Wilde wrote "The Ballad of Reading Gaol." With the alteration of but a single

word, certain stanzas of that tragic poem make a fitting epitaph
for John Jasper—murderer.

> "In Maidstone gaol by Maidstone town
>   There is a pit of shame,
> And in it lies a wretched man
>   Eaten by teeth of flame,
> In a burning winding-sheet he lies,
>   And his grave has got no name.
>
> And there, till Christ call forth the dead,
>   In silence let him lie:
> No need to waste the foolish tear,
>   Or heave the windy sigh:
> The man had killed the thing he loved,
>   And so he had to die."

The Genesis of "Edwin Drood"

(Part One)

T HIS IS the last night I have to live, and I will set down the naked truth without disguise. I was never a brave man, and had always been from my childhood of a secret, sullen, distrustful nature. I speak of myself as if I had passed from the world; for while I write this, my grave is digging, and my name is written in the black-book of death.   ⟡   ⟡   ⟡

The foregoing quotation might well have been taken from the end of the second part of *The Mystery of Edwin Drood*—that never-to-be-written portion of the novel that Charles Dickens carried with him to the grave. It suggests also the beginning of the review of John Jasper's career as outlined briefly by John Forster in his remarks concerning the novelist's disclosure to him of the plot for his last unfinished work. Actually, however, the sentences form the second paragraph of a short story appearing in *Master Humphrey's Clock*. Published as a serial in eighty-eight weekly issues from April 4, 1840, to November 27, 1841, this lesser-known collection of sketches and stories served as a framework for *The Old Curiosity Shop* and *Barnaby Rudge*. The short story in question bears the title, "A Confession found in a prison in the time of Charles the Second"; it is worth considering because it has so many resemblances to the fragment left by the novelist at his death. And these resemblances are so striking that I am forced to the conclusion that

"A Confession" was the germ that ultimately developed into the story we know today as *The Mystery of Edwin Drood*.

John Jasper, Edwin Drood's uncle and probable murderer, is not unlike the unknown author of "A Confession," whom I shall call the Narrator, and who describes himself as "of a secret, sullen, distrustful nature." Dickens, painting on a broader canvas with greater detail when he came to his last creative work, says of Jasper: "impassive, moody, solitary, resolute, so concentrated on one idea, and on its attendant fixed purpose, that he would share it with no fellow-creature, he lived apart from human life." Jasper was a lone wolf on a larger scale than the Narrator of "A Confession"; that is the only essential difference between the two men.

Both became guardians of their nephews, and the nephew of each was an orphan. The Narrator held a trust over a child of four; Edwin Drood was a young man approaching his majority.

Because the boy resembled his deceased mother, whom the Narrator hated, the latter gradually conceived a plan for murdering him. This plan, as he explains, coming by slow stages "to be part and parcel—nay nearly the whole sum and substance—of my daily thoughts, and resolving itself into a question of means and safety; not of doing or abstaining from the deed," grew in the Narrator's mind to the proportion of an *idée fixe*. John Jasper might in like fashion have echoed these words when he finally revealed his carefully matured design to do away with his "dear Ned," the only obstacle standing between him and Rosa Bud, the object of his passion.

"I never could bear that the child should see me looking at him, and yet I was under a fascination which made it a kind of business with me to contemplate his slight and fragile figure and think how easily it might be done. Sometimes I would steal upstairs and watch him as he slept." Thus wrote the Narrator, meditating upon his projected murder. John Jasper was equally fascinated by Edwin Drood, for whom he had what his nephew termed an almost "womanish" concern. "Once for all, a look of intentness and intensity—a look of hungry, exacting, watchful, and yet devoted affection—is always, now and ever afterwards, on the Jasper face whenever the Jasper face is addressed in this direction." And the Narrator's habit of stealing upstairs to watch the boy in slumber is perfectly matched by Jasper when he returns from the home of Minor Canon Crisparkle on the night of the famous quarrel between Edwin Drood and Neville Landless. "His nephew lies asleep, calm and untroubled. John Jasper stands looking down upon him, his unlighted pipe in his hand, for some time, with a fixed and deep attention."

The Narrator of "A Confession" murders his nephew when the child goes to a deep sheet of water to sail a toy boat—a lure fashioned by his uncle to entice the boy to this secluded spot. Having slain the child with his sword, he resolves to bury the body in his garden.

"I had no thought that I had failed in my design, no thought that the water would be dragged and nothing found." In like manner Jasper had no idea that his murder plan had failed solely because of the ring of diamonds and rubies carried by Edwin upon his person— the ring about which Jasper knew nothing, but which was destined in the end to bind and drag him to his doom. He had no idea that the river and its adjoining banks would be vainly searched for days, although he realized at once that no body would be forthcoming. The absence of a *corpus delicti* made Jasper's position desperate, since it enforced the eventual release from custody of Neville Landless, upon whom Jasper had worked long and craftily to fasten suspicion.

"I must encourage the idea that the child was lost or stolen," wrote the Narrator. "All my thoughts were bound up and knotted together in the absorbing necessity of hiding what I had done." How equally do those statements apply to Jasper, after old Hiram Grewgious had told him that Edwin and Rosa had broken off their engagement on amicable terms, agreeing to be to each other thereafter no more than brother and sister! To avert suspicion from

himself, the wretched choirmaster was compelled to suggest that
his nephew had gone away of his own volition.

"How I felt when they came to tell me that the child was missing, when I ordered scouts in all directions, when I gasped and
trembled at every one's approach, no tongue can tell or mind of
man conceive," the Narrator continued. For "scouts" we have only
to substitute the "placards and advertisements" that "should be
widely circulated imploring Edwin Drood, if for any unknown
reason he had withdrawn himself from his uncle's home and society, to take pity on that loving kinsman's sore bereavement and
distress, and somehow inform him that he was still alive." Jasper
likewise, when the murder of his nephew was no more than the
product of his feverish dreams, betrayed an anxiety similar to that
of the Narrator. Minor Canon Crisparkle is our witness to this fact:
"Long afterwards he had cause to remember how Jasper sprang
from the couch in a delirious state between sleeping and waking,
and crying out: 'What is the matter? Who did it?' "

The Narrator of the "Clock" story was sitting with his chair
actually upon the grave of his dead nephew on the fourth night
after the murder when he was visited by one who had served with
him abroad, accompanied by a brother officer. Their conversation
was soon interrupted by the appearance of two bloodhounds, which
tried to tear up the ground beneath the seat occupied by the murderer. His visitors called upon him to move, but he refused, order-
ing them to draw their swords and cut the dogs to pieces. At once
the officer sensed some mystery; the two men set upon the murderer
and forced him away, although he "fought and bit and caught at
them like a madman."

"What more have I to tell?" the Narrator concluded. "That I fell
upon my knees, and with chattering teeth confessed the truth, and
prayed to be forgiven. That I have since denied, and now confess
to it again. That I have been tried for the crime, found guilty, and
sentenced. That I have not the courage to anticipate my doom, or
to bear up manfully against it. That I have no compassion, no con-

solation, no hope, no friend.—That I am alone in this stone dungeon with my evil spirit, and that I die tomorrow."

Again, these closing words might have been uttered by John Jasper, who—according to information given John Forster by Dickens himself—was to have made a confession of his crime while in the condemned cell.

It is my contention that "A Confession found in a prison in the time of Charles the Second," written when Dickens was a comparatively young man, has all the essential features of the fragment he left us at his death: the murder of a nephew by his uncle; the secret burial of the body; a psychological similarity in the thoughts and actions of the murdering agents. In the monthly parts which were never to be written, we would undoubtedly have had the tracking down of the murderer of Edwin Drood, his capture, and his confession to the crime given from the death cell. The bloodhounds of the "Clock" manuscript have been replaced by the activities of Dick Datchery; the ring of diamonds and rubies delicately set in gold would have identified what remained of Edwin Drood's body. I have not the slightest doubt that, consciously or subconsciously, Charles Dickens had in mind this earlier product of his pen when he constructed his plot for *The Mystery of Edwin Drood*.

Thomas Wright states with reference to a story by Percy Fitzgerald, a young contemporary of Dickens and the novelist's friend: "Dickens thought as highly of Fitzgerald's work as he did of Mrs. Trollope's. He indeed, according to Mr. Kitton, altered the plot of *Edwin Drood* entirely, after reading *An Experience,* a story which Fitzgerald contributed to *All the Year Round*. 'It is,' says Dickens, on 19 August 1869, 'according to my thinking, one of the most remarkable pieces I ever saw!'—Whoever, therefore, wants to understand *Edwin Drood* and Dickens's attitude to it should not neglect Percy Fitzgerald's *An Experience*."[1]

Since I have been endeavoring over a period of years to fathom and understand the mysteries of the novel and Dickens's attitude

---

[1] *A Life of Charles Dickens* (London: H. Jenkins, 1935), pp. 341–342.

toward it, I have read and studied this story in two chapters which appeared in *All the Year Round:* No. 37, New Series, on Saturday, August 14, and Saturday, August 21, 1869. These dates are not without their significance, as will be seen from what follows. However, either Mr. Kitton or Mr. Wright (or possibly both) was in error when he stated that "An Experience" was written by Percy Fitzgerald. I am justified in making such an assertion by a letter Dickens addressed to Miss Emily Jolly, authoress of *Mr. Arle* and several other novels:

Office of All the Year Round
Thursday, Twenty-second July, 1869

Dear Miss Jolly,—Mr. Wills has retired from here (for rest and to recover his health), and my son, who occupies his place, brought me this morning a story[2] in MS., with a request that I would read it. I read it with extraordinary interest, and was greatly surprised by its uncommon merit. On asking whence it came, I found that it came from you!

You need not be told, after this, that I accept it with more than readiness. If you will allow me I will go over it with great care, and very slightly touch it here and there. I think it will require to be divided into three portions. You shall have the proofs and I will publish it immediately. I think so VERY highly of it that I will have special attention called to it in a separate advertisement. I congratulate you most sincerely and heartily on having done a very special thing. It will always stand apart in my mind from any other story I ever read. I write with its impression newly and strongly upon me, and feel absolutely sure that I am not mistaken.—Believe me, faithfully yours always.

That Dickens was indeed tremendously impressed by "An Experience" seems evident not only from what he wrote Miss Jolly but also from additional letters which I shall soon have occasion to reproduce. First of all, however, it would be well to remember that he had already turned his mind to the problem of *Edwin Drood,* if we are to believe John Forster when he says that "in the middle of July" he received the following query: "What should you think of the idea of a story beginning in this way?—Two people, boy and girl, or very young, going apart from one another, pledged to be

---

[2] "An Experience," which appeared on August 14 and 21.

married after many years—at the end of the book? The interest to arise out of the tracing of their separate ways, and the impossibility of telling what will be done with that impending fate?" "In the middle of July" certainly implies a date prior to the 22d, when Dickens first read Miss Jolly's manuscript.

It is unlikely that Miss Jolly declined the novelist's suggestion that he "touch" her story "here and there," for he wrote to his daughter Mary:

Office of All the Year Round
Tuesday, Third August, 1869

My dearest Mamie,—I send you the second chapter of the remarkable story. The printer is late with it, and I have not had time to read it, and as I altered it considerably here and there, I have no doubt there are some verbal mistakes in it. However, they will probably express themselves.

But I offer a prize of six pairs of gloves—between you, and your aunt, and Ellen Stone, as competitors—to whomsoever will tell me what idea in this second part is mine. I don't mean an idea in language, in the turning of a sentence, in any little description of an action, or a gesture, or what not in a small way, but an idea, distinctly affecting the whole story *as I found it.* You are all to assume that I found it in the main as you read it, with one exception. If I had written it, I should have made the woman love the man at last. And I should have shadowed that possibility out, by the child's bringing them a little more together on that holiday Sunday.

But I didn't write it. So, finding that it wanted something, I put that something in. What was it?—Your affectionate Father.

With his own novel still in mind, Dickens made a sportive little mystery of his addition to the story affecting him so strongly. And although there is no date for the ensuing brief note to W. H. Wills, he must have written it soon after the letter addressed to his daughter:[3]

26 Wellington Street, Strand, London, W. C.

My dear Wills,—

All goes well here. I have been "at it" considerably. Look at a very remarkable story in 2 chapters, An Experience, which begins next week.

---

[3] In a footnote to "Who Was Dick Datchery?" I had occasion to refer to *Charles Dickens as Editor, being letters written by him to William Henry Wills, his Sub-Editor,* selected and edited by R. C. Lehmann. This book, seen after the completion of the present study, showed me that what I had discovered in the third volume of letters edited by Mr. Walter

Finally, on August 6, he wrote to John Forster the famous letter in which he spoke of the change made in what was to become *The Mystery of Edwin Drood*. Forster does not reproduce—except as a footnote—the introductory part of this letter in his *Life of Charles Dickens;* since it contains an additional reference to Miss Jolly's story, I include it here:

I have a very remarkable story for you to read. It is in only two chapters. A thing never to melt into other stories in the mind, but always to keep itself apart—

—I laid aside the fancy I told you of, and have a very curious and new idea for my new story. Not a communicable idea (or the interest of the book would be gone), but a very strong one, though difficult to work.

The story, I learnt immediately afterward [Forster continues], was to be that of the murder of a nephew by his uncle; the originality of which was to consist in the review of the murderer's career by himself at the close, when its temptations were to be dwelt upon as if, not he the culprit, but some other man, were the tempted. The last chapters were to be written in the condemned cell, to which his wickedness, all elaborately elicited from him as if told of another, had brought him. Discovery by the murderer of the utter needlessness of the murder for its object, was to follow hard upon the commission of the deed; but the discovery of the murderer was to be baffled till towards the close, when, by means of a gold ring which had resisted the corrosive effects of the lime into which he had thrown the body, not only the person murdered was to be identified but the locality of the crime and the man who committed it. So much was told to me before any of the book was written; and it will be recollected that the ring, taken by Drood to be given to his betrothed only if their engagement went on, was brought away with him from their last interview. Rosa was to marry Tartar, and Crisparkle the sister of Landless, who was himself, I think, to have perished in assisting Tartar finally to unmask and seize the murderer.

It will be helpful to keep this summary of the plot of *Edwin Drood* in mind as we examine "An Experience." In view of Forster's account, I am inclined to believe that the novelist had all the essential features of the plot for his narrative well within his mental grasp before he read Miss Jolly's manuscript; certainly there is

---

Dexter for the "Nonesuch Dickens" was indeed a "brief note," as quoted above, since it was but a single paragraph from the actual communication. Mr. Lehmann, however, gives the entire letter, which bears the date: Tuesday, Third August, 1869.

nothing in her story remotely touching upon the Datchery assumption, for example. Nor is there anything in it bearing upon the main theme of the Drood novel: the study of the mentality and character of a rebel against society who becomes a murderer. But we shall find that certain situations of "An Experience" have more or less definite resemblances to episodes in *Edwin Drood*. Since it is impossible to ascertain just what parts of Miss Jolly's narrative represent Dickens's alterations, and these were considerable, there is no justification for assuming that he borrowed this or that situation similar to happenings in his own work. That he contributed a certain idea to the second chapter of the tale is evident from the letter to his daughter. I would infer that Dickens absorbed its atmosphere; that recollections of certain passages or situations, for which he may himself have been responsible, colored his treatment of the plot he had already evolved for *Edwin Drood*.

"An Experience" is told in the first person by one Bertram Dowlass, an ambitious, iron-nerved, hardheaded and hardhearted young surgeon. He is no sentimentalist, but boasts of his brain; he is proud of the fact that he has read hard and worked hard.

On an early June afternoon he meets in his consulting room, for the first time, a woman of corpselike pallor, with dark eyebrows, who is accompanied by a little girl some two or three years old. The child is lame. Although the woman complains that Dowlass is young to be a surgeon, he assures her that the child, whose eyes have an unusual effect upon him, can be cured. He advises the use of chloroform in the operation he considers necessary to effect the cure, but he is by no means certain that Dr. Fearnwell, his superior, will permit it. Dr. Fearnwell might tell the mother that her daughter's lameness would not kill, whereas the cure might very well be fatal. Dowlass assures her that the operation, if undertaken at all, will be performed within the week. The mother suggests that Dr. Fearnwell need not see her. Dowlass says that in any event the child must be examined by a council of surgeons.

Dr. Fearnwell is of the opinion that the child is too delicate for the proposed operation. Dowlass wins his point, however, by concealing the whole truth about the child, and the operation is scheduled for 11:00 A.M. on a Monday. The mother dreads the coming ordeal; her daughter is all she has left from the past. If death comes to her child, she will curse the hand of God or of the man who took her.

Dowlass has learned that the mother is a Mrs. Rosscar, and he is by no means impervious to her extreme beauty. Thinking of the coming operation, he takes a boat trip on the Sunday before the day when it is to be performed. On the boat he meets Mrs. Rosscar and the child; the mother informs him that she is taking the excursion to give her daughter fresh air. Dowlass offers to squire her. She accepts, telling him she will try to love God when her child walks again. He notes that Mrs. Rosscar is in mourning, but that her bearing is regal. They go out in a rowboat and dine together. Dowlass observes that Mrs. Rosscar is a *woman* and a lady.

"I believe," he says, "that, just at the time when I first met her, my brain was on the point of giving-in, and of resenting the strain of some years." He is unconsciously falling in love with Mrs. Rosscar.

The operation is performed upon the child, and is successful. Dr. Fearnwell, taking stock of Dowlass, tells him that he is overdoing things, and that he should go away on a vacation.

"I knew that late that day," Dowlass muses, "when I first saw Mrs. Rosscar after the operation, her expression of her passionate joy and gratitude made me half delirious with an uncomprehended feeling—and that part of it was *fear*."

The child is placed in a ward, where Mrs. Rosscar watches over it night and day. "The more radiant the mother's face was, and the more entirely all seemed well, the more I felt afraid."

On the third day after the operation, the child sinks and dies in its sleep. There was no reason why the little girl should not have lived, Dowlass declares, even though dominated by her mother.

"I resolved that I *would not* meet her eyes," he says, "but she was the stronger willed, and our eyes did meet. I shrank; I shivered; I looked, I know, abject, craven, self-convicted. I felt I was the murderer she thought me."

"As her lips opened, to give utterance to the first words of her curse, I, lifting my own arms, as if to ward off from my head an imminent blow (they told me afterwards of these things), and struggling for power to articulate some deprecation—I, meeting her eyes with unspeakable horror in my own, staggered a moment, then fell, as if she had struck me down."

This is the climax of the first chapter, and it inevitably suggests the dramatic moment in *Edwin Drood* when Hiram Grewgious informs Jasper that his nephew and Rosa had broken off their engagement prior to Edwin's disappearance. What follows will illustrate the parallelism. "Mr. Grewgious saw a ghastly figure rise, open-mouthed, from the easy-chair, and lift its outspread hands towards its head." "Mr. Grewgious saw the ghastly figure throw back its head, clutch its hair with its hands, and turn with a writhing action from him." "Mr. Grewgious heard a terrible shriek, and saw no ghastly figure, sitting or standing; saw nothing but a heap of torn and miry clothes upon the floor."

There is indeed a similarity between the two situations, but the superior power and artistry of Dickens are immediately apparent.

At the beginning of the second chapter of "An Experience," Dowlass regains consciousness only to find himself in his own rooms. It is nighttime, he notices, and still summer. A woman sits by him, sewing; somehow he senses that she is Mrs. Rosscar.

"That he may not die, great God, that he may not die!" Dowlass hears her pray, whereupon he knows *fear*.

"Why was I given over to her?" is the question that torments his mind.

She tells him that he has been ill for a month; he has been suffering from congestion of the brain. She has been nursing him ever since her child was buried. Dowlass again lapses into unconsciousness, remaining in that state for another week.

"For some time after I had got on a good way towards recovery," he says later, "I talked and thought of myself as 'that sick man': seemed to watch what was done for me, as if it were being done to some other person." Here is a striking parallelism to a part of Forster's remarks forming a commentary to the letter Dickens wrote him on August 6—the part in which he states that the originality of *Edwin Drood* "was to consist in the review of the murderer's career by himself at the close, when its temptations were to be dwelt upon as if, not he the culprit, but some other man, were the tempted."

On one of his visits to the sick man, Dr. Fearnwell informs Dowlass that he owes his life to his nurse. Later, Mrs. Rosscar tells her patient to call her "Huldah"; only one person has called her by that name since her childhood.

Speaking of his attitude toward the woman he now loves, Dowlass remarks: "I was under a spell of fascination not devoid of fear." His feeling, as quoted in his own words, is not at all unlike that entertained by Rosa Bud for John Jasper.

"I loved her with a desperate sort of passion," Dowlass exclaims as he probes his emotions more deeply. "A love far more of the senses than the heart."

"It was the beauty of her presence that so grew upon me: of her whole physical self, as it were. Of her mind and heart I knew nothing."

John Jasper might have said something very like this in analyzing his passion for Rosa; he too felt the appeal to the senses made by a lovely body. Did he not cry out to her as he stood by the sun dial in the garden of the Nuns' House: "How beautiful you are! You are more beautiful in anger than in repose. I don't ask you for your love; give me yourself and your hatred; give me yourself and that pretty rage; give me yourself and that enchanting scorn; it will be enough for me."

At last Dr. Fearnwell becomes impatient because Dowlass does not get well. He plans to remove the sick man to a farm where he will have a better opportunity to recover. At this point Mrs. Rosscar feels that she has to leave, but she promises to rejoin Dowlass later, at the farm, if he will not again expose her to Dr. Fearnwell's remarks. She suggests that she may appear there as Dowlass's sister.

She comes to him on the afternoon of the second day after his removal to the farm. Dowlass finally tells her of his love for her, then asks her to marry him.

"That *I* should love *you!*" she cries. "Is it credible?"

Later on she calls him in to the house. "My patient, you must come in, the dew begins to fall."

"Somehow," Dowlass confesses, "the way that hand touched my shoulder, and the slight accentuation on that word 'my,' made me shudder." Some recollection of that avowal may have found its way to Dickens's mind when he wrote the chapter describing the unaccountable nocturnal expedition made by Jasper and Durdles to the cathedral crypt and the great tower. Before the two men ascend the stairs leading to the summit of the tower, the stonemason tells Jasper how he sought refuge in the cathedral from some town boys who had set upon him when he was celebrating the holiday season on the night of December 24. "And here I fell asleep," he says. "And what woke me up? The ghost of a cry. The ghost of one terrific shriek, which shriek was followed by the ghost of the howl of a dog: a long, dismal, woeful howl, such as a dog gives when a person's dead. That was *my* last Christmas Eve."

On the following day, Dowlass and Mrs. Rosscar are outdoors, seated in some warm hay. Presently Dowlass falls asleep and has a weird dream. "My hand went quickly to my throat when I awoke, and there lay across it—nothing dreadful—only a heavy tress of Mrs. Rosscar's hair, which, slipping loose, had uncoiled itself as she bent over me."

There is undoubtedly a suggestion of strangulation in the sentence just quoted; the "heavy tress" of hair may have transformed itself at a later date into Jasper's great black scarf.

The two go into the house. Dowlass suggests that they visit the grave of Mrs. Rosscar's child. Here I may say that I am inclined to consider this visit to be the idea introduced by Dickens—the idea to which he referred in his letter to his daughter Mary. The influence produced by the graves of little children had a great effect upon Dickens; witness the amount of space he gives to the vigil kept by Little Nell's grandfather at her place of burial.

Mrs. Rosscar says she will accompany Dowlass to her daughter's grave only when she becomes his wife. Despite every argument she raises to the contrary, Dowlass insists upon marrying her.

The day is finally set for their marriage, but she bursts into tears when he pours out his passion for her before the fire.

They go to the child's grave. Once there, the mother in her will not let her carry out her plan.

"That evening she told me her history, and what had been her proposed revenge. She had designed to make me love her madly. That she had done. She had designed to let me marry her, who had been a mother and not a wife. She had designed, as the wife of my infatuated love and unspeakable passion, to have cursed me as her child's butcher, at her child's grave. She had designed—or was the nameless dread and horror of my illness taking this terrific form in its flight?—when she had thus slowly ground down my heart to its last grain of misery and grief, to murder me in my bed."

There is in the proposal just outlined a faint foreshadowing of Jasper's relentless dogging of Neville Landless. And does not Helena Landless say to Rosa, when they are together in Tartar's rooms after Rosa's flight to Hiram Grewgious, her guardian: "If Neville's movements are really watched, and if the purpose really is to isolate him from all friends and acquaintance and wear his daily life out grain by grain (which would seem to be the threat to you), does it not appear likely—that his enemy would in some way communicate with Mr. Tartar to warn him off from Neville?"

The rather unusual use of the word "grain," present in both works, strikes me as significant.

"I could have married you for hate," Mrs. Rosscar finally tells

Dowlass; "but for such love as has arisen in my soul for you—if indeed it is love, or anything but compassion and kindness towards the poor wretch I have helped back to life—never!"

She leaves him; Dowlass never sees her again.

It seems evident that "An Experience" impressed Dickens strongly enough to have exerted some influence, at least, on the plot development of *Edwin Drood,* as I have endeavored to show by the comments punctuating my brief summary of Miss Jolly's story. Coupled with the basic idea of "A Confession found in a prison in the time of Charles the Second," it enhanced the psychological and emotional setting of the unfinished novel. The spell of fascination tinged with fear exercised over Bertram Dowlass by Mrs. Rosscar foreshadows the hint of animal magnetism or hypnotism introduced now and again in *Edwin Drood;* I am convinced that Dickens meant to employ this phenomenon with even greater emphasis in the latter half of the work now existing only as a fragment. Such resemblances as exist between "An Experience" and the novel are not surprising when we recall that Dickens touched up or rewrote certain parts of the story, thereby making it in some degree his own creation.

The Genesis of
"Edwin Drood"

(Part Two)

BEFORE he had begun the actual composition of *Edwin Drood,*
Dickens had accepted for publication in *All the Year Round* a story
by Robert Lytton. The following letter gives further evidence of
the novelist's tendency to rewrite or touch up manuscripts scheduled
to appear in his magazine—a tendency justified not only by his
position as editor, but by the fact that articles and stories printed in
his publication did not bear their authors' signatures.

> Thursday, Second September, 1869
>
> My dear Robert Lytton,—John Acland [*sic*] is most willingly accepted, and
> shall come into the next monthly part. I shall make bold to condense him here
> and there (according to my best idea of storytelling), and particularly where
> he makes the speech:—And with the usual fault of being too long, here and
> there, I think you let the story out too much—prematurely—and this I hope to
> prevent artfully. I think your title open to the same objection, and therefore
> propose to substitute:
>
> The Disappearance
of John Acland.
>
> This will leave the reader in doubt whether he really *was* murdered, until the
> end.

Lytton's story—in thirteen chapters—began in *All the Year Round*
on Saturday, September 18, 1869, when chapter i was published. Its
official title was: *The Disappearance of John Ackland. A True
Story.* Subsequent installments of the tale appeared as follows:
Saturday, September 25, chapters ii, iii, iv; Saturday, October 2,

chapters v, vi, vii, viii; Saturday, October 9, chapter ix; Saturday, October 16, chapters x, xi, xii, xiii. As one may readily deduce from this schedule, the manuscript had been subjected to a great amount of compression. We shall soon learn that it underwent a sweeping condensation as well. The reason for the hurried presentation of this story is made clear by the letter Dickens wrote to Lytton:

Friday, October 1, 1869

My dear Robert Lytton,—I am assured by a correspondent that "John Acland" has been done before. Said correspondent has evidently read the story—and is almost confident in "Chambers's Journal." This is very unfortunate, but of course cannot be helped. There is always a possibility of such a malignant conjunction of stars when the story is a true one.

In the case of a good story—as this is—liable for years to be told at table—as this was—there is nothing wonderful in such a mischance. Let us shuffle the cards, as Sancho says, and begin again.

You will of course understand that I do not tell you this by way of complaint. Indeed, I should not have mentioned it at all, but as an explanation to you of my reason for winding the story up (which I have done to-day) as expeditiously as possible. You might otherwise have thought me, on reading it as published, a little hard on Mr. Doilly [sic]. I have not had time to direct search to be made in "Chambers's"; but as to the main part of the story having been printed somewhere, I have not the faintest doubt. And I believe my correspondent to be also right as to the where. You could not help it any more than I could, and therefore will not be troubled by it any more than I am.

The more I get of your writing, the better I shall be pleased.

Do believe me to be, as I am,

Your genuine admirer and affectionate friend.

J. Cuming Walters, in *The Complete Mystery of Edwin Drood,* makes the following comment on the letter given above and the situation leading Dickens to write it:

Dickens, in a letter written by him as editor of *All the Year Round,* explained to the Hon. Robert Lytton why he could not continue the publication of his story *John Acland* as originally projected. Dickens's letter was peculiarly apologetic in tone, and manifestly he desired to salve Lytton's wounded feelings; though obviously he had no alternative but to discontinue a story which he discovered "had been done before." But here follows the bewildering series of facts. The story of *John Acland,* begun in 1869, was of a man mysteriously murdered by his closest friend, his body untraced, his probable reappearance in the flesh suggested, the corpse ultimately discovered in an ice-house, and identity established by means of a watch. It is at once apparent that this plot closely resembles in outline the plot of *Edwin Drood*. Yet Dickens, finding the story had been "done before," stopped Lytton's story in 1869, and six months later began a similar one himself! On this the following queries arise:—

1. What was the original story that was so like Lytton's *John Acland,* and where is it to be found?

2. Are the parallels such as to suggest that Lytton copied them from that story, or are they merely coincidences?

3. Has any explanation been given why Dickens, knowing Lytton's work and aware of its similarity to another story, should at a later period decide to deal with the same theme?

In a previous study of *The Mystery of Edwin Drood*— "Who Was Dick Datchery?"—I referred to this "John Ackland" episode, basing my remarks on the passage quoted at length from Mr. Walters. At that time I was not familiar with the second letter written by Dickens to Robert Lytton, nor had I read the latter's story as it was published in *All the Year Round*. Now that I have read both letter and story, I find Mr. Walters somewhat misleading—to say the least—in his treatment of the whole situation. As I have already indicated, *John Ackland* was published as a complete narrative in five successive issues of Dickens's magazine, although its thirteen chapters were manifestly much condensed from their original form. When Walters says, "he could not continue the publication of his story *John Acland* as originally projected," the reader naturally infers that publication of the story was somehow suspended. And when Walters goes on to state that "he had no alternative but to discontinue a story which he discovered 'had been done before,' " the reader's inference that *John Ackland* was suspended is strengthened. Finally, when Walters asserts: "Yet Dickens ... stopped Lytton's story in 1869," the reader is certain that the tale was broken off before reaching its logical end. The truth of the matter was otherwise. Lytton's story was actually completed, so far as development of its plot through the denouement was concerned, even though it was undoubtedly rewritten and compressed.

There are other parts of Walters's passage which are likewise misleading. I do not agree with his assertion that the second letter to Lytton is "peculiarly apologetic" in tone. It is what Dickens himself would have called a "manly" letter, had he read it over the signature of another person. It is indicative of his greatness of heart that he, a busy editor in failing health, should have taken the time to write in a vein so considerate and reassuring. No doubt the letter did salve Lytton's wounded feelings—if indeed he felt wounded. I feel, however, that Dickens went out of his way to explain his justifiable action as editor, and that he did so because it was not in his nature to hurt anyone needlessly.

When Walters deals with the actual plot of *John Ackland,* he is more than misleading. He states that Ackland's body was "ultimately discovered in an ice-house, and identity established by means of a watch." He implies, of course, a parallelism with Edwin Drood's gold watch and chain, apparently flung into Cloisterham Weir to prevent identification of the young man's body by its means, and later found caught among the stakes of the weir by Minor Canon Crisparkle. The statement Walters makes is correct only in part. John Ackland—I have been using the spelling of the name as it appeared in *All the Year Round*—was indeed murdered and his body concealed beneath cakes of ice in an underground icehouse on a Virginia plantation. The murderer had shot him in the head, but his features were not mutilated; when his body—frozen and preserved—was finally brought to light, it was instantly recognized. His identity was not established by means of a watch, as Walters asserts. In point of fact, it was the murderer who was identified by Ackland's special chronometer, which he had stolen from the body of his victim and given to his daughter.

It is of course obvious that the plot of *John Ackland* bears some resemblance to that of *Edwin Drood,* just as the plots of both stories bear a resemblance to that of "A Confession found in a prison in the time of Charles the Second." But the latter antedates *John Ackland,* and no charge of plagiarism can logically be brought against an author who redevelops and amplifies a plot he has himself evolved years before. Futhermore, there is good reason for believing that Dickens must have had the essential features of the plot of *Edwin Drood* well in mind before he received from Robert Lytton the manuscript of *John Ackland*. It must have reached him shortly before September 2, when he wrote his letter of acceptance, whereas it was on Friday, August 6, 1869, that he wrote to John Forster about the "very curious and new idea for my new story." And Forster adds to his quotation from this letter the valuable information that he "learnt immediately afterward" what amounts to a résumé of all the salient points—minus the Datchery assumption—in the story of Edwin Drood. Any author who has ever attempted to write in the exacting medium of the detective story—or what the French call so picturesquely *le roman policier*—realizes full well that he can make no headway whatsoever unless he has at his fingers' tips and in chronological order every detail of his plot, intricate or otherwise. The final chapter, in which the detecting personality usually reveals how the murder, be it one or many, was committed and who was the guilty agent, must be distinctly present in his mind before he puts down his opening sentence. So must Dickens have had *Edwin Drood* in mind.

My reading of *John Ackland* convinces me that it had no real influence on the writing of *Edwin Drood,* and that its plot impressed Dickens far less than that of "An Experience." Take for example the second letter that Dickens wrote to Lytton on *John Ackland*. As editor of *All the Year Round* he had, for a legitimate reason, cut, condensed, and perhaps rewritten a good portion of the original manuscript. Yet he does not reproduce the chief character's name as it appeared in the proof sheets. Nor does he recall the correct spelling of the name of the watchmaker who acts as the detective in the Lytton narrative. He refers to him as "Mr. Doilly," whereas the text in *All the Year Round* has "D'Oiley," an oleaginous name far more in keeping with its owner's trade—and less suggestive of a table mat. I have not overlooked the obvious fact that both "D'Oiley" and "Datchery" begin with a "D" and end with a "y," but I attribute it to coincidence and not to intent.

Lastly, we learn from Forster's *Life* that Dickens "finished his first number of *Edwin Drood* in the third week of October, and on the 26th read it at my house with great spirit." Now Dickens could not have received the manuscript of *John Ackland* much before September 2, as I have said before. Whatever influence Lytton's story is presumed to have had on *Edwin Drood* must have made itself felt within the space of some eight weeks. Within this time Dickens would have been obliged not only to alter his plot as already outlined to Forster soon after August 6, but also to write on an entirely new basis the first monthly installment of his novel. *Edwin Drood* proves conclusively that no such procedure actually took place.

If any further evidence is needed to prove that Dickens was well aware of the plot for his last novel long before his acceptance of Lytton's manuscript, I submit an excerpt from a letter addressed to Sir Arthur Helps. The fact that it is dated Saturday, March 26, 1870, does not alarm me, for my contention that an author of mystery stories must know his *entire* plot before starting to write still holds.

I send you for Her Majesty the first number of my new story which will not be published till next Thursday, the 31st. Will you kindly give it to the Queen with my loyal duty and devotion? If Her Majesty should ever be sufficiently interested in the tale to desire to know a little more of it in advance of her subjects, you know how proud I shall be to anticipate the publication.

To the first two questions raised by Walters at the end of the passage I have quoted from him, I have no positive answers. Like Dickens, I have not had time to search for the original story so like *John Ackland,* a story supposed to be in *Chambers's Journal.* Therefore I am in no position to state whether the parallels are such as to suggest that Lytton copied from the story, or whether they are merely coincidences. With regard to the third question, I object first of all to the way in which it is framed. I do not admit that Dickens in *Edwin Drood* is dealing with the same theme as that

employed by Lytton in *John Ackland*. It is true that both men wrote
of the murder of a person whose body could not be found over a
long period of time; so of both stories the inevitable question was
raised: Was the man who had disappeared dead or alive? Indeed,
there have been (and no doubt still are) some enthusiastic followers
of Edwin Drood who believe that he was not murdered, and that
he would have returned to confront his wicked uncle had Dickens
only lived to finish the novel. We know that John Ackland actually
was murdered, whereas we can never know with absolute certainty
that Edwin Drood met a like fate. But apart from this similarity in
plot which, to my way of thinking, lies "in the public domain," the
finished *John Ackland* and the unfinished *Edwin Drood* are as
antipodal as night and day. As between *John Ackland* and "A Confession found in a prison in the time of Charles the Second,"
Dickens's incomplete fragment more nearly resembles the latter,
his own creation. Perhaps Dickens himself realized this fact, and
it is altogether possible that he shortened the original version of
John Ackland and hurried its publication because it bore a certain
resemblance to his plot for *Edwin Drood,* upon which he was even
then at work. I say "possible" as a mere conjecture—but not probable, for I believe that his second letter to Lytton expresses the whole
truth of the matter. I have not answered Walters's question as he
framed it, but I have tried to give him my explanation of the situation.

It might be well to consider at this point the selection of the title
for the novel whose inception we are considering, since it has, in
my opinion at least, some bearing on the plot. Dickens was always
in some degree of torment until he had decided upon a definite title
for a new story. Forster gives much interesting information about
his difficulties in naming some of the earlier novels, but we must
turn to the few private notes for *Edwin Drood,* discovered after
Dickens's death, to find the list of tentative titles jotted down by the
novelist for his last work. They are as follows, under date of Friday,
August 20, 1869.

1. The Loss of $\begin{smallmatrix} \text{James} \\ \text{Edwyn} \end{smallmatrix}$ Wakefield.
2. James's Disappearance.
3. Flight and Pursuit.
4. Sworn to Avenge It.
5. One Object in Life.
6. A Kinsman's Devotion.
7. The Two Kinsmen.
8. The Loss of Edwyn Brood.
9. The Loss of Edwin Brude.
10. The Mystery in the Drood Family.
11. The Loss of Edwyn Drood.
12. The Flight of Edwyn Drood.
13. Edwin Drood in Hiding.
14. The Loss of Edwin Drude.
15. The Disappearance of Edwin Drood.
16. The Mystery of Edwin Drood.
17. Dead? or Alive?

The word "loss" occurs in five out of the seventeen tentative titles, "disappearance" twice, and "mystery" twice. If Dickens had any conception of what his plot was like before he listed these possible titles for his new book—and he must have had, in view of the date assigned to his notes,—then it would seem evident that Edwin Drood (to use his name in its final form) was destined to be lost. The word "disappearance" likewise bears out such a conclusion, although perhaps the sense of finality is not so great. It may be remembered that, in his first letter to Lytton, Dickens suggested that the "disappearance" of John Ackland would prevent readers from discovering whether he really *was* murdered until the end. The word "mystery," ultimately a part of the title chosen by the novelist, is the vaguest and least revealing of the three; it does, however, succeed more adequately in challenging the reader's interest. And in a letter to Bulwer Lytton, dated Monday, May 20, 1861, Dickens said something pertinent with reference to this word "mystery," the one he himself finally used: "As to title, 'Margrave, a Tale of Mystery,' would be sufficiently striking. I prefer 'Wonder' to 'Mystery,' because I think it suggests something higher and more apart from ordinary complications of plot, or the like, which 'Mystery' might seem to mean." Certainly *The Mystery of Edwin Drood* has a complicated plot; so we may consider Dickens's final choice of key word a fitting one.

The third title in the list would seem to refer to Rosa's flight from Jasper, after he had revealed his passion for her in the garden at the Nuns' House, and to Jasper's pursuit of her and Neville Landless. Dickens may have rejected this entry because it dealt with too restricted a part of his story.

Titles 4, 5, and 6 tend to bear upon John Jasper, and all three of them—especially the last two—have a slightly ironical twist of meaning.

Number 7 is rather colorless; it lacks the startling quality which Dickens may well have desired in the title of a novel such as he intended *Edwin Drood* to be.

Numbers 12 and 13 are undoubtedly the ones dearest to the hearts of those Droodians who insist that Edwin was not murdered, and that he was to reappear and confront Jasper. And yet the key word of number 12 might refer to the soul's flight—Dickens used three quotations from *Macbeth* in his novel,—while "in hiding" admits of an interpretation favorable to the belief that young Drood was murdered. If Jasper had chosen a burial place for the reception of his nephew's body with such skill that it was beyond all possibility of being discovered, then his victim would assuredly have been "in hiding" for all time.

I do not mean to imply by my comments that anything in the way of a definite solution to the riddles in *Edwin Drood* may be deduced from these tentative titles, of which only the sixteenth was actually chosen, but I do believe that they reflect to some degree the workings of Dickens's mind as he formulated his plot. Some of them clearly indicate the "loss" or "disappearance" of Edwin Drood, without, however, revealing Dickens's meaning of the terms; whereas others hint at the importance of John Jasper's role in the story. I have not as yet mentioned the seventeenth entry; but coming at the last, as it does, it puts strikingly the very question that Dickens undoubtedly wanted his readers to ask themselves: Was Edwin Drood really murdered, or did he survive? Dickens alone could have answered this query, but death intervened before he was ready to do so. As long as the fragment he left is read and studied, that question will always arise.

It so happens that there is something else to consider in the genesis of *The Mystery of Edwin Drood,* and this I now give to the reader for what it is worth. Again I turn to J. Cuming Walters and to his book entitled *Clues to Dickens's 'Mystery of Edwin Drood.'* " In it we find Walters saying:

> As further bearing out the fact that it was actual murder that was to be the basis of the plot, and not an attempt at murder that failed, it should be remembered that in Rochester itself, which is Cloisterham, a real event is believed to have provided Dickens with his idea. The story is given in W. R. Hughes's "Week's Tramp in Dickens-land." A well-to-do person, a bachelor, was the guardian and trustee of a nephew (a minor), who was the inheritor of a large property. The nephew went to the West Indies and returned unexpectedly. He suddenly disappeared, and was thought to have gone on another voyage. The uncle's house was near the site of the Savings Bank in High Street, and when excavations were made years later the skeleton of a young man was discovered. The local tradition is that the uncle murdered the nephew, and thus concealed the body. Here is the germ of the plot of "Edwin Drood," and the mystery is not so much the nature of the crime as its concealment and eventual detection.

The result of such research as I have made is now before the reader. There are, as possible influences on the plot development of *Edwin Drood,* "A Confession found in a prison in the time of Charles the Second," "An Experience," *The Disappearance of John Ackland,* and the Rochester tradition. It might almost seem time to raise the old cry, "You pays your money and you takes your choice"—yet there is something more to be said. For there is still one last factor to be considered, one of greater importance than any number of literary influences: the creative genius of Charles Dickens.

He was fifty-seven and a half years old when he began to work out the plot of what proved to be his last novel, and he was to leave

that novel an unfinished fragment and an abiding mystery. Broken
in health, haunted by approaching paralysis, weakened by the
cumulative strain of more than four hundred public readings at
home and abroad, with their attendant difficulties of almost constant
travel under arduous circumstances, he yet had the driving urge to
create something new in the way of literary art, whose devoted
servant he had been for so many years. Miss Gladys Storey pene-
trates to the heart of the matter in her fascinating book of reminis-
cences, *Dickens and Daughter*, when she says:

> Those who have studied the character of Charles Dickens in all its varying
> phases and moods, where strength, weakness, tenderness, severity, generosity
> and carefulness are revealed, and take their places beside other traits of
> character in this so extraordinary and wonderful a man, will recognize that
> the dominant characteristic lying behind every trait which, with hurricane
> force, swept through his entire mental and physical being, was his amazing
> energy, at times demoniacal in its fierceness.

And this energy found its highest form of expression in the exacting
field of literary creation. Dickens himself acknowledged this fact in
these words:

> I hold my inventive capacity on the stern condition that it must master my
> whole life, have complete possession of me, make its own demands upon me,
> and sometimes for months together put everything from me. If I had not
> known long ago that my place could never be held unless I were at any
> moment ready to devote myself to it entirely, I should have dropped out of
> it very soon.

And so, driven by the power of this amazing creative energy, he
began *The Mystery of Edwin Drood* under most adverse conditions
of health and physical well-being. That there was in his own mind a
recognition of the fact that he was entering a race against the
shadow of death is manifest from the unusual clause he caused to
be inserted in the contract for his last novel.

> That if the said Charles Dickens shall die during the composition of the
> said work of THE MYSTERY OF EDWIN DROOD, or shall otherwise become in-
> capable of completing the said work for publication in twelve monthly num-
> bers as agreed, it shall be referred to John Forster, Esq., one of Her Majesty's
> Commissioners in Lunacy, or in the case of his death, incapacity, or refusal to

act, then to such a person as shall be named by Her Majesty's Attorney-General for the time being, to determine the amount which shall be repaid by the said Charles Dickens, his executors, or administrators, to the said Frederic Chapman as a fair compensation for so much of the said work as shall not have been completed for publication.

Despite his poor health, he was handling a theme big in scope, and handling it in masterly fashion. The story was, I believe, in some ways to suggest *The Moonstone,* which Dickens meant to rival and surpass. It was to suggest Meadows Taylor's *Confessions of a Thug,* which Dickens had read. But above all, it was to contain something unusual and surprising—"a very curious and new idea." The reader's interest was to be aroused not only by the mystery of Edwin Drood's disappearance and the Datchery enigma, but also by the riddle of the nature of John Jasper himself.

Now Dickens had always been fascinated by murderers; he gave himself wholly to his portrayal of Bill Sikes in his reading—or rather enacting—of the housebreaker's brutal murder of Nancy. Even against the advice of both friends and physicians, he made that gruesome and frightfully realistic portrayal a part of his reading program again and again, until at last he was forced by failing health to abandon the platform forever.

But his fascination for murderers still persisted, and of all those he created—Bill Sikes, Jonas Chuzzlewit, Mr. Rudge, and Bradley Headstone, to mention but a few—John Jasper is by far the most absorbing. And just as he went back to *Oliver Twist* for the reading that offered the greatest challenge to his tremendous energy and drained it most, so I believe he turned to the story from *Master Humphrey's Clock* to find the initial inspiration for the development of his plot for *Edwin Drood.* The vast difference between "A Confession found in a prison in the time of Charles the Second" and the unfinished last novel is a true measure of the steady growth of his creative genius.

The very heart and soul of *The Mystery of Edwin Drood* is, in the last analysis, John Jasper himself. In essence, the novel is a study of the warped mentality of a rebel against society, a rebel with whom Dickens associated himself. I make this statement out of my firm conviction that Dickens in his later years had come to feel that he was a lone individual who somehow stood outside the social framework and moral code which we term Victorian. After extolling the solid virtues of normal family life, he had put away his wife and broken up his own home. Hoping for a kind of companionship he had never known, he had fallen desperately in love with an eighteen-year-old actress, Ellen Lawless Ternan, who became his mistress after the formal deed of separation from his wife had been put into effect. He had been almost ruthless in his endeavor to capture a fresh lease on life and love, but the realization of his impetuous desire fell short of what he had anticipated. All that we need to know about this tragic episode in the life of Dickens has been revealed in Thomas Wright's biography and in Miss Gladys Storey's *Dickens and Daughter*. As Miss Storey says, quoting Mrs. Perugini (Kate Dickens): "My father was like a madman when my mother left home; this affair brought out all that was worst—all that was weakest in him. He did not care a damn what happened to any of us. Nothing could surpass the misery and unhappiness of our home." And we read, farther on: "Everybody and everything became subservient to the furtherance of the object he had irrevocably set out to accomplish, which sad business took eight months to complete, from the day of the final performance of the play at Manchester. In his anguish, Dickens wrote to Wilkie Collins: 'I have not known a moment's peace or contentment, since the last night of *The Frozen Deep*. I do not suppose that there ever was a man so seized and rendered by one spirit.' "

He had sinned against the moral code of the social class in which he had moved, although he was not by birth one of its members, as one to the manner born, esteemed and respected. Ever conscious of the dark period of poverty, menial labor, and practically no prospect of further education which had wrung his soul in childhood, always fearful lest he should not earn enough money to maintain himself and his large family in a style befitting the position he had achieved, he had acted circumspectly until his affair with Miss Ternan. When he became a self-made rebel against the prevailing conventions of his day, he must indeed have felt alone. And so he lost himself in the characters of his own creation, and poured out his waning energy in his portrayals of those intensely real though fictitious men, women, and children who had brought laughter to the lips and tears to the eyes of his hosts of readers. At the end of his robust life, when he began the writing of *Edwin Drood,* he was to plumb the emotional depths of a man who had killed the thing he loved, even as he himself had destroyed something once very dear to him. John Jasper, too, was "seized and rendered by one spirit":—his passion for Rosa Bud. So intense was that passion that he swore he would pursue the object thereof even "to the death." In like manner Dickens had pursued the object of his passion to the death of all that might otherwise have made him the happiest of mortals. Therefore I cannot escape the conviction that John Jasper and Charles Dickens are, in a sense, one person by virtue of the same sort of literary sublimation that had made David Copperfield the *alter ego* of his creator.

In his presentation of the choirmaster, lay precentor, and opium addict whom we know as John Jasper, Dickens was attempting a psychological study more penetrating than any he had previously undertaken, because it was a searching of his own soul. John Jasper is the Narrator of the *Clock* manuscript, broadened, deepened, and intensified to the utmost degree by the strong emotions which Dickens had himself experienced. The short story, written so many years before, is but a faint, melodramatic foreshadowing of the greater and more human opus, so tragically cut in half by its author's untimely death.

Was Edwin Drood Murdered?

(PART ONE)

H E STROLLS about and about, to pass the time until the dinner-hour. It somehow happens that Cloisterham seems reproachful to him to-day; has fault to find with him, as if he had not used it well; but is far more pensive with him than angry. His wonted callousness is replaced by a wistful looking at, and dwelling upon, all the old landmarks. He will soon be far away, and may never see them again, he thinks. Poor youth! Poor youth!

◇ ◇ ◇

These lines, taken from the fourteenth chapter of *The Mystery of Edwin Drood,* epitomize the life of the young engineer whose mysterious disappearance forms the basis of the present study. With an enigmatic heading for this chapter wherein Edwin Drood goes up the postern stair to his uncle's lodgings and to that fateful dinner on Christmas Eve, Charles Dickens raised a question that has not yet received a final answer. "When shall these Three meet again?" he called it; by "these Three" he meant Neville Landless, Edwin Drood, and John Jasper. As every reader of the unfinished novel knows, Edwin Drood was never seen again after that night. Was he murdered by his uncle Jasper, who had evidently been plotting to do away with his nephew because of his own passion for Rosa Bud, Edwin's fiancée since childhood, or did he somehow escape his uncle's evil designs and come back to Cloisterham in that half of the novel which Dickens was never to write? I shall present the evidence of the story itself, together with the testimony of several contemporaries of Charles Dickens, to persuade the reader that there can be but one answer to the question: Edwin Drood died the victim of a murderous attack by his uncle.

I have said that the lines quoted at the beginning of this study epitomize the life of Edwin Drood. They are a picture in little of the young man as we know him in what would doubtless be one-third of the novel's length, had it reached completion. Young Drood strolls about and about, to pass the time until the dinner hour, just as he traveled between London and Cloisterham to see his fiancée and to pass the time until they should be married and set forth for Egypt, where he hoped to make a name for himself in his profession. Cloisterham reproaches him even as Rosa did, for the young couple were unhappy in their relationship, forced upon them by their respective fathers. The cathedral town finds fault with him, just as Rosa did; is more pensive than angry, as was Rosa. His break with his fiancée has chastened his easygoing nature and made something of a man of him, but he is marked for death. And in the last four words of the passage, Charles Dickens virtually writes his epitaph.

"Poor youth! Poor youth!" Lest any reader should interpret these words as an exclamation of self-pity arising in Edwin's own mind, let me set down here the sentence Dickens originally wrote to follow: "He will soon be far away, and may never see them again, he thinks." I am indebted to Mr. Percy Carden for the information that the manuscript of the novel, housed in the Victoria and Albert Museum in South Kensington, London, goes on as follows: "Ah, he little knows how near a case he has for thinking so." Surely here is a comment made by Dickens himself—a comment he evidently considered too revealing of what was to come, since he replaced it by the briefer: "Poor youth! Poor youth!" I contend that Dickens was fully aware of the fate in store for Edwin Drood, and that he intended the young man to meet death at the hands of his uncle.

Probably the outstanding exponent of the theory that Edwin Drood was to escape the murderous attack of his uncle Jasper and live to confront him in the unwritten portion of the novel was Richard A. Proctor. His famous book, *Watched by the Dead: A Loving Study of Dickens's Half-told Tale,* appeared in 1887; in it he developed at the outset an argument best expressed in his own words: "The idea which more than any other had a fascination for Dickens, and was apparently regarded by him as likely to be most potent in its influence on others, was that of a wrong-doer watched at every turn by one of whom he has no suspicion, for whom he even entertains a feeling of contempt." And on the very next page of his study he adds: "It became a favorite idea of Dickens to associate the thought of death either with the watcher or the watched; and, unless I mistake, in the final and finest development of his favourite theme, he made one 'dead and buried as all men supposed' watch the very man who supposed him dead, and not only buried but destroyed." In other words, Proctor argues that Edwin Drood returns to Cloisterham in the guise of Dick Datchery and ultimately tracks Jasper to his doom.

Now Mr. Proctor cites examples to bolster up his contention. In *The Old Curiosity Shop,* Sampson and Sally Brass are watched by the Marchioness; in *Martin Chuzzlewit,* Jonas Chuzzlewit is watched by Nadgett, and Pecksniff is watched by old Martin Chuzzlewit; Dombey, of *Dombey and Son,* is under the calculating eye of Carker; Carker in turn is watched by old Mother Brown and her daughter. In *Bleak House,* Mademoiselle Hortense is watched by Inspector Bucket's wife. In *Little Dorrit,* Rigaud is dogged by Cavalletto. Magwitch watches Pip in *Great Expectations,* while Compeyson watches Magwitch. And so it is only natural, argues Proctor, that John Jasper should be watched by Edwin Drood. But Proctor evidently failed to observe that Jasper is watched by Hiram Grewgious, whom I believe to be Dick Datchery, by the Opium Woman, and by Deputy. Nor does he appear to be aware of how relentlessly John Jasper spied upon Neville Landless.

Speaking of Edwin Drood at a later point in his study, Proctor states: "There is not one note of death in aught that he does or says. As the time approaches for Jasper's attack on him, there is much in the music of the story to suggest that trouble is approaching; but he is not to die, albeit the reader is to think him dead. The music of his words was under Dickens's control in the same sense that the timbre of his natural voice was under his control. He might disguise it more or less successfully, according to the quality of his hearer's audition; he could not really change it. So he does all he can to conceal by his words the ideas which, nevertheless, the sound of his voice suggests to those who have ears to hear."

With all due respect for Proctor, I consider most of what he says to be mere assertion, and I still contend that Edwin Drood was marked for death. I admit that he does not do or say anything that hints at his approaching end. How could he, since he was entirely unaware of his uncle's slowly maturing plan to murder him? But what does Dickens himself say with regard to young Drood? When John Jasper goes in quest of Durdles on the night of their unaccountable expedition to the cathedral crypt and tower, Dickens has this to say in his description of the old stonemason's yard: "The two journeymen have left their two great saws sticking in their blocks of stone; and two skeleton journeymen out of the Dance of Death might be grinning in the shadow of their sheltering sentry-boxes, about to slash away at cutting out the gravestones of the next two people destined to die in Cloisterham. Likely enough, the two think little of that now, being alive, and perhaps merry. *Curious, to make a guess at the two;—or say one of the two!*" (The italics are mine.) Does not Dickens refer to Edwin Drood in those last words? Why should the reader be invited to make a guess at two—or one (with an exclamation mark)—if they or he be utter strangers to the story? There is no point to Dickens's suggestion unless he is hinting at Edwin's ultimate fate.

Again, in the chapter entitled "Both at their Best," wherein Edwin and Rosa agree to break off their irksome engagement and become as brother and sister, Dickens says, with reference to young Drood: "He called her Pussy no more. Never again." Now we know that Hiram Grewgious took Edwin to task for referring casually and openly to his sweetheart by this endearment; the old lawyer held: "A name that it would be a privilege to call her by, being alone with her own bright self, it would be a liberty, a coldness, an insensibility, almost a breach of good faith, to flaunt elsewhere." Supposing Edwin to have recalled the old lawyer's reproach on that score, we might understand that he called Rosa "Pussy" "no more," even though he was alone with her on the occasion in question. But "Never again" is a redundancy. It smacks of too much emphasis—unless Dickens had some hidden meaning behind the forceful reiteration. In that case, it becomes suggestive of finality. I maintain that the "Never again" is the novelist's way of informing the reader that Edwin was soon to die. Had he lived to marry Rosa—the broken engagement having undergone repair,—he would undoubtedly have called her Pussy in their fonder moments, and "Never again" would have been deliberately misleading.

I do not understand too clearly what Proctor means when he says: "The music of his words was under Dickens's control in the same sense that the timbre of his natural voice was under his control. He might disguise it more or less successfully, according to the quality of his hearer's audition; he could not really change it. So he does all he can to conceal by his words the ideas which, nevertheless, the sound of his voice suggests most clearly to those who have ears to hear." If I were to paraphrase the pasage just quoted, I should do so in the following manner: "Dickens could write sentences expressing clearly his fundamental ideas, just as he could say what he actually meant. He might change his voice sufficiently to deceive an inept listener, although his voice would be essentially the same. So he does all he can to write sentences in such a way that the reader will be deceived about their real meaning—but an acute observer and student of the novelist's style will see through the subterfuge and grasp the true meaning of these sentences."

In other words, Proctor seems to imply that when Dickens writes a passage apparently conveying the idea that Edwin Drood is to die, he really does not mean that at all; he really means that Drood is to live. Whether or not Proctor actually does mean that the novelist could write certain sentences embodying this literary sleight of hand, and so convey one meaning to the ordinary reader at the same time that he offered something vastly different to those of keener perception, I shall leave for my own readers to judge. If they deem that to be the idea underlying this rather obscure bit of writing, let me quote a later portion of Proctor's argument and consider its validity in the light of two passages taken from *Edwin Drood*.

Proctor says of Rosa: "She learns from Grewgious, before Cloisterham knows anything about it, that Drood has been the victim of a terrible and murderous attack, but has been saved as by a miracle; and she has had it earnestly impressed upon her that she is not to show by word or deed that she knows of Drood's safety. Later she is to wear mourning for him, as dead. But Mr. Grewgious keeps carefully from her the knowledge that the man who loves her so hatefully is the man who would have slain her once affianced lover, still loved as a dear brother. That she should remain in ignorance on this point is essential to Mr. Grewgious's and Edwin Drood's plans for punishing Jasper." I do not understand how Proctor can make such an assertion when the following passages, written by Charles Dickens, are considered. When Neville Landless is taken before Mayor Sapsea and examined at length after Minor Canon Crisparkle's discovery of Edwin's watch and chain on Cloisterham Weir, Dickens writes: "Even the broad suggestion that the lost young man had absconded, was rendered additionally improbable on the showing of the young lady from whom he had so lately parted; for, what did she say, with great earnestness and sorrow, when interrogated? That he had, expressly and enthusiastically, planned with her, that he would await the arrival of her guardian, Mr. Grewgious. And yet, be it observed, he disappeared before that gentleman appeared." This is an abstract of Rosa's testimony, and

Dickens has certainly concealed from me by his artful use of words
any idea that Rosa had learned from Grewgious that Edwin has
been the victim of a terrible and murderous attack from which he
has been saved as by a miracle. If her sorrow and earnestness on this
occasion are feigned, as Proctor must inevitably assume, then she
possessed histrionic ability not to be deduced from Dickens's portrayal of her.

Similarly, when Jasper has his interview with Rosa in the garden
of the Nuns' House, Dickens says: "She cannot look up at him for
abhorrence, but she has perceived that he is dressed in deep mourning. So is she. It was not so at first; but the lost has long been given
up, and mourned for, as dead." If Proctor is correct in his assumption that Rosa knows Edwin to be alive, and that she is playing a
part to enable her erstwhile fiancé and Grewgious to carry out their
plans for punishing Jasper, why did she not wear mourning from
the start? Why was it assumed only at a later date? And how could
Dickens add the words "and mourned for" and still play fair with
his readers? Those words are indicative of Rosa's personal feelings,
and we are to infer—if I can understand plain English—that she
actually felt sorrow and grief for the man to whom she was once
affianced, and that she truly believed him to be dead.

No, I am afraid that Proctor fell in love with a tempting theory,
and so overlooked a great deal of straightforward writing on the
part of Dickens. Evidence that this conclusion is valid is the complete falsity of a statement he makes on page 77 of his study: "Mr.
Grewgious was to dine with Rosa on Christmas day." What are the
facts of the situation? The whole question of the visit comes up
when Grewgious calls upon Rosa at the Nuns' House to sound her
out on her attitude with regard to her eventual marriage to Edwin.
"Could I," Rosa asks, at the close of their conversation, "could I ask
you, most kindly to come to me at Christmas, if I had anything
particular to say to you?"

"Why, certainly, certainly," Grewgious replies. "As a particularly
Angular man, I do not fit smoothly into the social circle, and con-

sequently I have no other engagement at Christmas-time than to partake, on the twenty-fifth, of a boiled turkey and celery sauce with a—with a particularly Angular clerk I have the good fortune to possess, whose father, being a Norfolk farmer, sends him up (the turkey up), as a present to me, from the neighbourhood of Norwich. I should be quite proud of your wishing to see me, my dear."

All of which merely signifies that Grewgious *would* break his engagement if Rosa were to send for him.

What actually happens? When Rosa and Edwin have their final talk resulting in the amicable breaking off of their engagement— and this is on Friday, December 23, because Edwin tells her: "I dine with the dear fellow [his uncle] tomorrow and next day—Christmas Eve and Christmas Day,"—Rosa says: "My guardian promised to come down, if I should write and ask him. I am going to do so."

Now she could not have written her letter to Grewgious before Friday evening, for Dickens tells us that "the bright, frosty day declined as they walked and spoke together. The sun dipped in the river far behind them." And she could not reasonably have posted her letter before Saturday morning, December 24, in which case it certainly would not have reached Grewgious, who resided in London, in time to enable him to come to Cloisterham on Christmas Day. Furthermore, we know from Rosa's testimony given before Sapsea that Edwin disappeared prior to the old lawyer's arrival in Cloisterham. Therefore I conclude that Proctor is in error, and that Grewgious dined with his clerk, Bazzard, as he had originally planned.

Again Proctor says, with reference to the startling news given to Edwin's uncle by the old lawyer after he has at last reached Cloisterham in response to Rosa's letter: "Jasper learns that he has murdered Drood uselessly, and, murderous villain though he is, he is horrified." I must remark in passing that I cannot comprehend Proctor's use of the verb form "murdered" or of the term "murderous villain" if he really believes Edwin to be alive. He goes on: "But it does not seem to have been noticed that Grewgious has no special reason, unless he is certain that Jasper believes himself to be the murderer of Drood, for supposing that Jasper will be startled by the news he brings. Yet he does suppose so." I imagine that Proctor arrives at this conclusion because he has said of Grewgious on a preceding page: "It is *absolutely impossible* that he can have any information justifying his cruel tone with Jasper, except from Drood himself."

When we examine the actual text of the novel, Proctor's argument falls to pieces. We find that Grewgious does have some information justifying his tone with Jasper; he does have a special reason for supposing that his news will surprise the choirmaster. As the old lawyer himself says upon this very occasion: "I have just left Miss Landless." And note that he makes this revealing statement only after the dialogue which I now reproduce:

JASPER: Have you seen his sister?
GREWGIOUS: Whose?
JASPER: The suspected young man's. [Jasper refers to Neville Landless.]
GREWGIOUS: Do you suspect him?
JASPER: I don't know what to think. I cannot make up my mind.
GREWGIOUS: Nor I. But as you spoke of him as the suspected young man, I thought you *had* made up your mind. —I have just left Miss Landless.

We learn that Grewgious has talked with Helena Landless, who is well aware of Jasper's passion for Rosa. She has learned of this passion from Rosa's own lips; she knows how abhorrent it is to her young friend. And when Helena and her brother had their talk with Minor Canon Crisparkle by the river, Helena exclaimed, after the good man had urged Neville to apologize to Drood for the quarrel which took place between the two young fellows in Jasper's rooms: "O Mr. Crisparkle, would you have Neville throw himself at young Drood's feet, or at Mr. Jasper's, *who maligns him every day?*" (The italics are mine.) Can we doubt, then, that Helena has poured out her heart to the old lawyer in defense of her brother, or that she has told him all she knows about Jasper? It is as much a certainty as though Dickens had informed us of the fact in so many words. Here, then, is Grewgious's justification for adopting his "cruel tone" with Jasper.

And we may be just as certain that Rosa has informed Grewgious of her interview with Edwin—else why did she write to her guardian?—and of the mutual breaking off of their engagement. This conclusion is confirmed by what Grewgious says to Jasper later on in this dramatic scene:

"One of this young couple, and that one your nephew, fearful, however, that in the tenderness of your affection for him you would be bitterly disappointed by so wide a departure from his projected life, forbore to tell you the secret, for a few days, and left it to be disclosed by me, when I should come down to speak to you, and he would be gone. I speak to you, and he is gone.

"I have now said all I have to say: except that this young couple parted, firmly, though not without tears and sorrow, on the evening when you last saw them together."

Here is ample evidence that the old lawyer has received Rosa's complete confidence, and that she has revealed to him all that transpired between her and Edwin. Will such news be no surprise to Jasper, who is so desperately in love with Rosa that he has committed murder to remove the obstacle existing between him and the object of his passion? We must give Grewgious credit for some shrewdness, even if Proctor does not. And when Jasper refers to Neville as "the suspected young man," what must be the old lawyer's conclusion? It is my contention that he suspects Jasper of the murder of his nephew, that he sees through the whole plot, but that he remains silent because there is no evidence—direct or circumstantial—to bring against the choirmaster so long as there is no *corpus delicti*. And it is obviously because of what is in his mind that he refuses to sit down and eat with the man whom he considers to be a murderer.

I have digressed to some extent from the main purpose of this study, that purpose being to answer the question, Was Edwin Drood murdered? Yet in a sense I have not gone too far afield, for I believe

I have shown beyond a reasonable doubt that Proctor's theory is not irrefutable; that Edwin Drood may reasonably be assumed to have met his death at the hands of his uncle. One more reference to *Watched by the Dead,* and I shall have done with Proctor. The grand climax of his work comes on page 166 when he says: "Jasper was to have been tracked remorselessly to his death by the man whom he supposed he had slain. Risen from his grave, Drood was to have driven Jasper to his tomb, there to seek for the dreaded evidence of his guilt; but to find there instead, alive and implacable, the man whom he had doomed to a sudden and terrible death, and in whose dust he had come to seek for the dreaded evidence of his guilt."

Such a conclusion is the logical outcome of Proctor's entire argument, but unfortunately it does not square with all the evidence obtainable from the text—evidence that proves decisively that Edwin Drood died on the night of December 24–25, murdered by his uncle, John Jasper.

Among all the various and varied commentaries I have read on *Edwin Drood,* I have yet to find one emphasizing the fact that John Jasper was a *young* uncle. Yet there can be no doubt about it, for Dickens informs us that Mr. Jasper was "a dark man of some six-and-twenty, with thick, lustrous, well-arranged black hair and whiskers." It has occurred to me that the novelist had a definite reason for making Edwin's uncle a man whose age span was but a few years longer than that of his nephew. And I have always pictured Jasper as a lean, wiry man possessed of considerable strength—perhaps because of the admirable illustrations drawn by Sir Luke Fildes to accompany the text; perhaps, too, because the lustrous black hair and whiskers are somehow indicative of virility. If Jasper is indeed the murderer of his nephew, as I firmly believe, there is every reason why he should have been endowed by his creator with comparative youth; he could not have been many years older than Edwin if he were to deal with his nephew in a physical contest such as might arise out of an attempt at murder by the means Jasper was planning to employ. And comparative youth—plus virility—was needed by Dickens in his conception of the choirmaster to make plausible the latter's intense passion for Rosa Bud, a mere schoolgirl still in her teens. Jasper's lust for his pupil, stronger than the undoubted deep affection he felt for his nephew, forms the basic motive for the murder of Edwin; it was inevitable, given Jasper's age and temperament, that the promptings of the flesh should overcome those of the spirit.

I feel very strongly that Dickens gave his readers a direct hint that Jasper was to be the agent of his nephew's death. When Miss Twinkleton addresses her young ladies on the day following the heated quarrel between young Landless and Edwin Drood, she alludes to "the immortal SHAKESPEARE, also called the Swan of his native river, not improbably with some reference to the ancient superstition that that bird of graceful plumage—*sang sweetly on the approach of death.*" (The italics are mine.) In similar fashion, on December 24, when the sands of Edwin's life are running out, John Jasper sings "sweetly on the approach of death." Dickens makes the implication clearly: "Mr. Jasper is in beautiful voice this day. In the pathetic supplication to have his heart inclined to keep this law, he quite astonishes his fellows by his melodious power. He has never sung difficult music with such skill and harmony, as in this day's Anthem. His nervous temperament is occasionally prone to take difficult music a little too quickly; to-day, his time is perfect."

Helena Landless recognizes in John Jasper a potential murderer, or I am much mistaken in the meaning underlying certain of her references to him. I have already had occasion to comment on her speech to Minor Canon Crisparkle: "O Mr. Crisparkle, would you have Neville throw himself at young Drood's feet, or at Mr. Jasper's, who maligns him every day?" And shortly afterward, when the Minor Canon urges the twin brother and sister to acknowledge openly the wrong done by Neville—a wrong they both acknowledge instinctively,—Helena asks: "Is there no difference between submission to a generous spirit"—meaning Crisparkle's—"and submis-

sion to a base or trivial one?'" It is certain that she has Jasper in mind
as a base spirit, whereas Edwin is one of a trivial sort. And still later,
when Rosa has fled from Jasper's detested lovemaking and taken
refuge with her guardian in London, Helena voices her opinion of
the choirmaster in even stronger terms. The two young women
have met in Tartar's rooms, and as they are about to separate after
their heart-to-heart talk, Rosa pleads: "Tell me that you are sure,
sure, sure, I couldn't help it."

"Help it, love?" prompts Helena.

"Help making him"—Jasper—"malicious and revengeful. I
couldn't hold any terms with him, could I?"

"You know how I love you, darling," answers Helena, with indignation; "but I would sooner see you dead at his wicked feet."

Yet it is Rosa herself, achieving maturity as a result of the ordeal
through which she has passed, who entertains the deepest suspicion
of Jasper; who realizes only too well the motive impelling her
music master to murder. With a precision which makes impossible
any acceptance of Proctor's theory that Rosa had been told by her
guardian that Edwin was still alive, Dickens reveals the confusion
existing in her mind throughout the six months that had elapsed
since the young man's disappearance. "A half-formed, wholly un-
expressed suspicion tossed in it, now heaving itself up, and now
sinking into the deep; now gaining palpability, and now losing it.
Jasper's self-absorption in his nephew when he was alive, and his
unceasing pursuit of the inquiry how he came by his death, if he
were dead, were themes so rife in the place, that no one appeared
able to suspect the possibility of foul play at his hands. She had
asked herself the question, 'Am I so wicked in my thoughts as to
conceive a wickedness that others cannot imagine?' Then she had
considered, Did the suspicion come of her previous recoiling from
him before the fact? And if so, was not that a proof of its baseless-
ness? Then she had reflected, 'What motive could he have, according to my accusation?' She was ashamed to answer in her mind,
'The motive of gaining *me!*' "

What of the other persons who were closely connected with Edwin Drood and his uncle? How did they feel about John Jasper? In the final chapter of the fragment—the last one he was ever to set down on paper—Dickens tells us: "The dreadful suspicion of Jasper, which Rosa was so shocked to have received into her imagination, appeared to have no harbour in Mr. Crisparkle's." Notice the use of the word "appeared," which introduces an element of doubt. "If it ever haunted Helena's thoughts or Neville's, neither gave it one spoken word of utterance. Mr. Grewgious took no pains to conceal his implacable dislike of Jasper"—the adjective employed by Dickens is forceful,—"yet he never referred it, however distantly, to such a source." Without stating it in a forthright way, Dickens gives us here, I am convinced, a list of those persons who deep down in their hearts suspected Jasper of the murder of his nephew.

It should now appear with some degree of clarity that Edwin Drood was murdered, and that John Jasper was his murderer. What, then, was the method selected by the choirmaster to destroy the young man who had become his rival? Dickens gives several references to strangulation, the way in which Edwin Drood was done to death—and hints at a secret burial place, since such a grave alone provides a reason why there was no *corpus delicti*. Without taking up space to locate the exact points in the novel where these references appear, I shall list them, and let them speak for themselves. The italicized parts of the excerpts are my own.

1. Then he comes back, pounces on the Chinaman, and seizing him *with both hands by the throat,* turns him violently on the bed.

2. . . . . whether they were ever *walled up* alive in odd angles and jutting gables of the building for having some ineradicable leaven of busy Mother Nature in them which has kept the fermenting world alive ever since.

3. *Tiresome old burying-grounds!* . . . And then there was Belzoni, or somebody, dragged out by the legs, half-*choked* with bats and dust. All the girls say: Serve him right, and hope it hurt him, and wish he had been quite *choked.*

4. *"You are not going to be buried in the Pyramids,* I hope?"

5. "And as to Belzoni, I suppose he's dead;—I'm sure I hope he is—and how can his legs or his *chokes* concern you?"

6. "How do you do, Mr. Edwin? *Dear me, you're choking!*"

7. ... and the daring Miss Ferdinand had even surprised the company with a sprightly solo on the comb-and-curl-paper, until *suffocated* in her own pillow by two flowing-haired executioners.

8. " 'Cos I ain't-a-goin' to be lifted off my legs and 'ave my braces bust and be *choked;* not if I knows it, and not by 'Im."

Surely these passages indicate a preoccupation, on the part of the author, with strangulation, and numbers 1 and 8 have to do with Jasper, who murdered his nephew by that method—who used his great black silk scarf as the instrument of his crime. There is likewise apparent in the portions of the story I have quoted briefly a hint that Edwin's body will be walled up in some monument—the Sapsea tomb, to be more specific, in the burial ground adjacent to Cloisterham cathedral.

I have saved one particular reference to strangulation for special consideration, since I believe it to be of deeper significance than all the others combined. One of the most famous chapters in the fragment Dickens left us is the twelfth: A Night with Durdles. Herein we find the gripping account of that "unaccountable expedition" made by Jasper in company with the old stonemason to the cathedral crypt; herein we see the two men ascend the great tower. That Dickens himself considered this chapter to be of unusual importance is evidenced by a note he set down beneath its title in his "Number Plans"—a memorandum intended for his eyes alone. And what was the tenor of this note? "Lay the ground for the manner of the murder, to come out at last."

Of all the theories I have read in explanation of this chapter and note, I consider that of Professor Henry Jackson to be not only the most interesting but the most original. It may be found in the third part of his unusual book: *About Edwin Drood*. I should like to quote a few sentences from that part, and I shall endeavor to select them in such a way as to do no injustice to Jackson's logical presentation of his ideas.

Surely this "unaccountable expedition" [he says], made with Durdles on Dec. 19, is a rehearsal of "the journey" which, as we have seen, Jasper proposes to make, and actually makes, with the indispensable fellow traveler: and presumably the study of the rehearsal will enable us to anticipate some details of the tragedy. From the top of the tower Jasper "contemplates the scene, and especially that stillest part of it which the Cathedral overshadows." Presumably one of his purposes is to estimate the suitability of the Close for murder and concealment. But I think that the estimate formed is unfavourable. . . .

Let us suppose then that Jasper, as he walks to and fro "among the lanes of light," finds a mound of lime similar to that which Durdles in his yard had described as "quick enough to eat your boots: with a little handy stirring, quick enough to eat your bones." To make away with the body of the victim would be better than to deposit it where it might be found: Durdles' hammer could do nothing against a heap of lime: and no casual passer-by could watch what was done in the crypt. The scheme is now complete. Drood, under the influence of strong drink, is to be flung or pushed down the winding staircase of the tower, and his body is to be deposited in a mound of quicklime in the crypt of the cathedral. Moreover, Jasper has made himself acquainted with the route which he is to take: he has ascended and descended the staircase, and has noted the places where Durdles stumbled: he has observed the effects produced upon Durdles by the strong drink: having, no doubt, already taken an impression of the key of the iron gate, he has now taken one of the key of the crypt: somewhere in the crypt he has discovered a heap of quicklime. In short, with Durdles for *corpus vile,* Jasper has rehearsed in all its details "the journey," that is to say, the ascent of the tower, which he is to make with Edwin on the following Saturday, Dec. 24. "The expedition" of Dec. 19 is then for us no longer "unaccountable."

My theory is then, in brief, as follows. When Drood returned to the gate-house not long after midnight on Christmas Eve, Jasper, having hospitably pressed upon him some of his "good stuff," proposed a visit to the Cathedral tower, and Drood was nothing loth. As they descended the staircase of the tower, Jasper threw his scarf over Drood's head, and, having thus silenced, blinded, and disabled him, pushed him down the steep stairs. Drood, if he was not killed, was stunned by the fall. Jasper dragged the body into the crypt, and, having removed from it the watch and the shirt-pin, buried it in the heap of quicklime.

In the closing pages of his book Jackson states: "Mr. Cuming Walters and Mr. Charles think that Drood did *not* escape, and I agree with them."

While I disagree in many respects with the conclusions reached by Jackson, as will be seen if one consults my earlier remarks on "John Jasper—Murderer," yet I am impressed by the originality of

his theory and by his painstaking attention to every small detail.
I have quoted at some length from *About Edwin Drood* because so
brilliant an interpretation shows just how cleverly Dickens concealed the real answer to the question raised by that brief note written for his own guidance: What was "the manner of the murder, to
come out at last"?

Professor Jackson failed to find that answer, I believe, as have
many others. I myself failed to discover it when I was writing my
study of Edwin Drood's uncle. The twelfth chapter is so masterly
a piece of atmospheric writing that the answer, coming as it does
at the end—"at last"—is entirely overlooked. And Dickens had
method in his reiteration of the phrase: "an unaccountable expedition." He thereby fixed the reader's attention so firmly on the activities of Jasper and Durdles while they were in the cathedral crypt
and on the summit of the great tower that the "manner of the murder" made no impression when it was actually revealed. The paragraph describing the ascent of the tower is written with so much
power that it still lingers in the reader's mind as he hurries on to
the end of the chapter. The account of Durdles's dream weaves a
similar spell; it gives an added impact to the imagination already
deeply stirred by the climb up the winding staircase and the journey
through strange places.

And so, with his consummate artistry, Dickens concealed "the
manner of the murder" until the end—although he had hinted at
it often enough, as I have already shown. Jasper and Durdles have
left the precincts of the cathedral, and each is about to turn homeward when Deputy yelps out his "Widdy widdy wen" jargon, and
pelts them with stones. And now let the master speak in his own
words:

" 'What! Is that baby-devil on the watch there!' cries Jasper in a
fury: so quickly roused, and so violent, that he seems an older devil
himself. 'I shall shed the blood of that impish wretch! I know I shall
do it!' Regardless of the fire, though it hits him more than once,
he rushes at Deputy, collars him, and tries to bring him across.

But Deputy is not to be so easily brought across. With a diabolical insight into the strongest part of his position, he is no sooner *taken by the throat* than he *curls up his legs,* forces his assailant to hang him, as it were, and *gurgles in his throat,* and *screws his body,* and twists, as *already undergoing the first agonies of strangulation."* (The italics are mine.)

Why, at this particular point, did Dickens indulge in a detailed—one might almost say, a clinical—analysis of "the first agonies of strangulation"? There was no real need of it, for the average reader is inclined, in my opinion, to be rather fond of the impish Deputy, and Jasper's assault on the boy is as unnecessarily brutal as is the description of its attendant torture. Certainly the scene did not result from any sadistic element in the novelist's nature. No, with all due apologies to Professor Jackson, it is Deputy—not Durdles—who is Jasper's *corpus vile*. It is Deputy who enacts for the reader what Edwin Drood is to suffer at the gatehouse on that momentous night of December 24–25 when his uncle, made wiser by his experience with Deputy's reactions, comes upon his nephew from behind, to throttle him with his great black scarf. Surely here is the "ground for the manner of the murder, to come out at last."

Was Edwin Drood Murdered?

(Part Two)

IT SEEMS perfectly clear to me that Charles Dickens meant Edwin Drood to meet his death at the hands of John Jasper, his uncle. There is something about the youth's very name that suggests his untimely extinction. Edwin Drood: the dull alliterative recurrence of the "d's" is like so many clods thumping down on a plain wooden coffin; the odd surname holds a brooding sense of doom, a suggestion of dread and death. I suppose we shall never know to what degree Catherine Dickens, herself a Scotchwoman, made her husband cognizant of Scottish words. But to me, at least, it is rather significant that the noun "droud"—similar in sound if not in spelling to Edwin's family name—is Scottish for "a codfish; a dull, lumpish fellow."

In a certain sense Edwin Drood really is a dull sort of fellow, with the swaggering self-assurance and self-importance characteristic of young men who have the impulsive enthusiasms of youth without the experience of maturity to control and direct them. In my study "Who Was Dick Datchery?" I have directed attention to the fact that Dickens never describes young Drood with the same careful detail as he does the other characters in the novel; he does emphasize his youth, and he shows by implication that Edwin was not gifted with a quick, perceptive mind. When young Drood is first introduced to us upon his visit to his uncle, Dickens stresses these traits, as the two passages that follow will show.

As the boy (for he is little more) lays a hand on Jasper's shoulder, Jasper cordially and gaily lays a hand on *his* shoulder—

Laying an affectionate and laughing touch on the boy's extended hand, as if it were at once his giddy head and his light heart, Mr. Jasper drinks the toast in silence.

I have always felt that the physical characteristics of Edwin, deftly characterized though he is, were slurred over by Dickens because the novelist knew that the youth was soon to disappear from the scene. With his great creative genius, Dickens could make a memorable figure of the veriest supernumerary, but Edwin appears more like a cog requisite to the mechanism of the novel's plot than any other person in the fragment. Even the firm of which Edwin's father was a former partner, and upon which the young man himself was a charge until he should come of age, never evinced—so far as we know—the slightest concern about a future shareholder when Edwin disappears. Whether this is an oversight on the part of Dickens, or whether the firm relied upon Mr. Grewgious to supply them with such information as might come to light concerning young Drood's whereabouts, is a matter for speculation. At any rate, we cannot feel—nor do I believe Dickens intended us to feel— any deep or lasting sorrow when Edwin is blotted out of the picture.

The young man was not, however, without honorable intentions; had he lived, he would have returned the ring of diamonds and rubies—the ring gifted with such power "to hold and drag"—to old Hiram Grewgious. And assuredly he would never have allowed Neville Landless to remain under a cloud of suspicion as the probable agent of his disappearance had he been in a position to come forward and clear young Landless. Dickens makes such assumptions logical beyond the shadow of a doubt, if one will but consider the passages listed hereafter:

1. He had a conscience.
2. He must either give the ring to Rosa, or he must take it back.
3. "I will be guided by what she says, and by how we get on," was his decision, walking from the gatehouse to the Nuns' House. "Whatever comes of it,

I will bear his words in mind [Edwin here refers to Mr. Grewgious] and try
to be true to the living and the dead."

4. And now, Edwin Drood's right hand closed again upon the ring in its
little case, and again was checked by the consideration: "It is certain, now,
that I am to give it back to him; then why should I tell her of it?"

5. He would restore them [the jewels] to her guardian when he came down.

Dickens's repeated emphasis on Edwin's firm intention to return
the ring to Grewgious can have no *raison d'être* unless we are to
infer that the young man could not keep his pledge to make such
restitution because he was dead. His complete silence in regard to
the all-important jewel proves his death.

There is something else that does so as well—something I have
never seen mentioned in any work I have read concerning this most
fascinating of mysteries. I suppose most readers of the novel are
aware that there is a break of six months in the time pattern of the
story shortly after Edwin has disappeared. Chapter xvii begins with
the words: "Full half a year had come and gone, and Mr. Crisparkle
sat in a waiting-room in the London chief offices of the Haven of
Philanthropy, until he could have audience of Mr. Honeythunder."
To the best of my knowledge, only once before in his writing career
did Dickens have recourse to any such lapse of time; that was in
Barnaby Rudge. It might be interesting to look into these two situations more closely, endeavoring to establish, if possible, the reasons
underlying the two time lapses.

In the case of *Barnaby Rudge,* which opens in the year 1775, we
shall have no difficulty in finding a solution to our problem. We
learn from John Forster with regard to this novel that, "begun
during the progress of *Oliver Twist,* it had been for some time laid
aside; the form it ultimately took had been comprised only partially
within its first design." We likewise discover that it was begun
before the end of January, 1841. In February of the same year, Dickens writes to Forster that he is relying on Grip the raven, and the
Varden household, to arouse interest in his story. In March, the pet
raven lending the novelist inspiration for Grip sickens and dies.
In June, mention is made to Forster of Lord George Gordon; in

September, Dickens writes of the prison riots. The novelist had closed chapter xxxii of *Barnaby Rudge* in the following abrupt and autocratic manner: "And the world went on turning round, as usual, for five years, concerning which this Narrative is silent." With chapter xxxiii we are ushered in upon a wintry evening in 1780, and are soon plunged into the Gordon Riots.

Now it is not difficult to deduce that Dickens had not originally meant to use these riots as material for his novel, and that the lapse of five years was imposed upon him by virtue of necessity if he wished to be historically accurate when he did introduce them. Seeing their dramatic possibilities, he decided to feature them, and so took the leap forward in time.

Such is not the case, however, when we turn to *Edwin Drood,* for no historical event plays a part in the action of the story. As Professor Jackson so ably demonstrated, Dickens follows a closely knit and fairly evident time schedule up to the seventeenth chapter, wherein we have a lapse of fully half a year. I have puzzled a good deal over this curious fact, for which there seems no obvious reason. Even the action of the story has been suspended to a considerable degree during these six months, although this hiatus does not particularly impress a reader who is not overcritical or analytical.

It was only while I was making a vain search for some authoritative explanation of the action of quicklime on a cadaver that a possible solution of the problem occurred to me. Tempting though it was, since it afforded additional proof that Edwin Drood was dead, I still felt the necessity of obtaining accurate information concerning quicklime and its effect on a body, for this knowledge I deemed fundamental to the whole situation. I had come to the conclusion that Dickens considered the six months' time lapse an absolute essential if he were to make reasonably certain an important factor in his plot; to achieve this result, he had to proceed on the assumption that within six months the quicklime used by John Jasper in the secret burial of his victim had completely destroyed the youth's body. But was his assumption scientifically sound?

Making a final attempt to settle this question, I presented my problem in a letter addressed to Dr. Alan R. Moritz, a criminal pathologist and head of the Department of Legal Medicine at Harvard Medical School. A week later I received a highly informative reply from Robert P. Brittain. Just how greatly indebted I am to him and to Dr. Moritz will appear from the paragraphs which, with permission, I now quote.

The answer to your principal question can be given categorically. A body buried in quicklime over a period of six months would not be entirely obliterated or even nearly so. This applies not only to the bones but to the "soft parts"—muscles and internal organs.

It may be of interest to you to have a little more background on this matter. It is a common belief that lime, especially in the form of quicklime, causes rapid destruction and dissolution of the body. Experiments have been carried out which show that this is not so. Theory here coincides with practice. There are a number of elements which play a part in normal putrefaction, the chief of which are moisture, presence of bacteria, and the presence of air. Quicklime absorbs moisture from the air or soil and from the body—forming slaked lime; it acts as an antiseptic and restrains the growth of bacteria; its physical presence helps to exclude air and by causing minor burning and drying of the body surface it tends to prevent free access of air to the deeper tissues. It may, further, effect a combination with fatty tissues—again increasing resistance to putrefaction.

In brief, quicklime does not hasten decomposition and any action it has on this process is in the other direction.

The Crippen Case which occurred in England in 1910 is of particular interest in this regard. Dr. Crippen murdered his wife and buried her in quicklime on or about the 31st of January. Disinterment took place on July 13. The body had been cut in pieces and parts were missing (not by dissolution), but the remainder was in a fair state of preservation. Hair also was found and clothing with the maker's name still legible on it, and a skin scar was identifiable.

I cannot help but remark at this point that the interval between the burial of Mrs. Crippen and the disinterment of her body closely approximates the six months' time jump in "The Mystery of Edwin Drood." Surely this is a striking coincidence between fact and fiction.

Lime has been used by other murderers either in the mistaken belief that it would destroy the body or to absorb and conceal odors. Cases are those of Manning and of Wainwright. In the latter chloride of lime was used.

Dr. Moritz has perused this letter and concurs with it.

From my study of the plot structure of the novel as we have it today, and in view of the detailed information contained in the letter from which I have quoted at length, I am forced to the conclusion that Dickens entertained the common but entirely erroneous belief that quicklime was capable of completely destroying a body, and that he acted upon such a belief when he planned and wrote *The Mystery of Edwin Drood*. That John Forster was of the same opinion is evidenced by his reference to the plot of the novel as Dickens outlined it to him: "all discovery of the murderer was to be baffled till towards the close, when, by means of a gold ring which had resisted the corrosive effects of the lime into which he had thrown the body, not only the person murdered was to be identified but the locality of the crime and the man who committed it." I am likewise convinced that the novelist, mistaken though he was with respect to the actual properties of quicklime, felt that he had made acceptable, through the six months' time lapse, the total obliteration of Edwin Drood's remains. If he had not gone upon such an assumption, Dickens would never have written what he did about the ring of diamonds and rubies—the one object carried by Edwin Drood upon his person of which John Jasper had not the slightest inkling; the only existing clue to the secret burial place and identity of the lost youth:—"Among the mighty store of wonderful chains that are for ever forging, day and night, in the vast iron-works of time and circumstance, there was one chain forged in the moment of that small conclusion [Edwin's decision not to speak of the ring to Rosa], riveted to the foundations of heaven and earth, and gifted with invincible force to hold and drag." Thus the novelist foreshadows the highly important part the ring is to play in the ultimate solution of the mystery.

Finally, the interest which Edwin Drood had begun to take in

Helena Landless impresses me as indirect proof that he was to die. Dickens refers to the young man's feeling on no fewer than three separate and distinct occasions. First mention of it is made when Edwin Drood and Neville Landless fall into bitter conversation on their way home after escorting Rosa and Helena to the Nuns' House: "Now, there are these two curious touches of human nature working the secret springs of this dialogue. Neville Landless is already enough impressed by Little Rosebud, to feel indignant that Edwin Drood (far below her) should hold his prize so lightly. Edwin Drood is already enough impressed by Helena, to feel indignant that Helena's brother (far below her) should dispose of him so coolly, and put him out of the way so entirely."

Again, when Edwin and Rosa have agreed to terminate their engagement and be henceforth as brother and sister, Dickens says: "And yet there was one reservation on each side; on hers, that she intended through her guardian to withdraw herself immediately from the tuition of her music-master; on his, that he did already entertain some wondering speculations whether it might ever come to pass that he would know more of Miss Landless."

And finally, when we follow Edwin Drood through the streets of Cloisterham on December 24, as he "strolls about and about, to pass the time until the dinner-hour" at the gatehouse, we read: "Though the image of Miss Landless still hovers in the background of his mind, the pretty little affectionate creature [Rosa], so much firmer and wiser than he had supposed, occupies its stronghold. . . . And still, for all this, and though there is a sharp heartache in all this, the vanity and caprice of youth sustain that handsome figure of Miss Landless in the background of his mind."

I have said that this preoccupation with Helena Landless is indirect proof of Edwin's death, for it does not reveal its full significance until it is linked with the later love affair developing between Rosa and Lieutenant Tartar, and with the deepening respect and love that Helena Landless feels for Minor Canon Crisparkle. If in some miraculous fashion Dickens had brought Edwin back to life in that second half of the novel he was destined never to write, there would have been no woman to be young Drood's mate. These twists and turns of the complicated plot had their purpose; John Forster knew whereof he spoke when he wrote: "Rosa was to marry Tartar, ,and Crisparkle the sister of Landless."

Some persons might argue that there is not much "mystery" to the novel if it is a foregone conclusion that Edwin Drood is murdered by his uncle; if we have only the ultimate tracking down of an identified murderer and his punishment to anticipate. In that event, they might ask, what is the significance of the story's title: "The Mystery of Edwin Drood"? My answer would be that there is still something more than meets the eye in this last unfinished creation of the genius we know as Charles Dickens. The "mystery" was more than a personal matter, more than a puzzle involving Edwin Drood and the circumstances of his disappearance; it embraced as well the most dominating factor in the young man's life— his uncle. Shakespeare called his great tragedy of passionate love and jealousy *Othello,* but what would that drama have been without Iago, who is the dark dynamic force that sets the tragedy in motion? So it is with *Edwin Drood*. Dickens was, in my opinion, far more concerned with the character and mentality of John Jasper—for reasons I have stated in an earlier study—than with the mystery pertaining to young Drood. The world was once shocked by the callous brutality of the Lindbergh kidnapping—yet some time elapsed before it was realized that the central figure behind that frightful crime was an obscure carpenter. The mystery of Edwin Drood's disappearance would have been solved, I believe, only when the greater mystery of the complex mind of his murderer had been fully revealed—had fate permitted—by the skill of the novelist.

It has been my endeavor to show how the novel itself proves, if I have interpreted it correctly, that Edwin Drood was done to death by his uncle. What is the testimony of Dickens himself in this respect, as well as that of persons who were closely connected with

him, and who had some information about his last novel? When
I speak of Dickens and the evidence we may obtain from him, I
have in mind the fragmentary notes he jotted down for guidance in
the development of his plot, chapter by chapter, as he wrote his
story. I acknowledge my indebtedness to W. Robertson Nicoll
for these notes, reproduced in his book *The Problem of "Edwin
Drood": A Study in the Methods of Dickens.* Under chapter ii,
"A Dean and a Chapter Also," we find: "Uncle & Nephew. Murder
very far off." Again, under chapter xii, "A Night with Durdles,"
we have that significant sentence already discussed in this study:
"Lay the ground for the manner of the murder, to come out at
last." Finally, there are the intriguing entries under chapter xvi,
"Devoted": "Edwin disappears. THE MYSTERY. DONE ALREADY."
Now it is inconceivable to me that Dickens, setting down these
notes for his own use, unaware that they would ever be seen by the
eyes of others, should have referred to a "murder" if he had no
more than the intention of writing about a murderous attack that
somehow failed of its purpose. That would have been carrying his
natural desire to keep his plot secret to an unnatural and exagger-
ated degree of caution. He had no reason whatsoever to deceive
himself. It must be remembered also that the notes quoted under
chapter xvi come after: "Jasper's Diary. 'I devote myself to his
destruction.'" Montagu Saunders has argued brilliantly that in so
devoting himself John Jasper was actually putting a noose about
his own neck. In my study, "John Jasper—Murderer," I have added
some amplifications to Saunders's theory, which I staunchly support. And so we may safely assume that Charles Dickens intended
Edwin Drood to be murdered, and that his uncle was to be his
murderer.

The testimony of John Forster—for years one of Dickens's most
intimate friends—bears me out in such an assumption. After quoting part of the famous letter he received from the novelist on
Friday, August 6, 1869, Forster adds: "The story, I learnt immediately afterward, was to be that of the murder of a nephew by his

uncle." It has been disputed whether Forster received his information by letter or by word of mouth from Dickens himself. The
arguments need not concern us here; in either case, Forster speaks
with authority of "the murder of a nephew by his uncle." And in
his subsequent remarks he gives a brief but comprehensive outline
of the basic plot of the story, without, however, referring to the
Datchery assumption. His authority has been questioned more than
once, of course, but it seems illogical to suppose that Dickens withheld the truth of the matter from him. Had he done so, Forster
would inevitably have detected some discrepancy between the information he received and the novel as he heard it read from the
manuscript prepared for publication in monthly parts.

> He finished his first number of *Edwin Drood* in the third week of October
> [1869], and on the 26th read it at my house with great spirit.
>
> At my house on New Year's Eve he read to us a fresh number of his *Edwin
> Drood.*
>
> And on the 25th [of February, 1870], when he read the third number of
> his novel.
>
> And on 21 March, when he read admirably his fourth number.
>
> On the night (7 May) when he read to us the fifth number of *Edwin Drood.*

Thus wrote John Forster in his biography of Dickens.

I have no hesitation in accepting Dickens's old friend as a reliable
witness to support my contention that Edwin Drood was murdered,
for the novelist's own daughter Kate, who became Mrs. Charles
Allston Collins, and later Mrs. Perugini, gives Forster an excellent
reputation for honesty. In an article in the *Pall Mall Gazette* for
June, 1906, entitled "Edwin Drood and Dickens's Last Days," she
made the following comments:

> It was not upon the Mystery alone that [my father] relied for the interest
> and originality of his idea. The originality was to be shown, as he tells us, in
> what we may call the psychological description the murderer gives us of his
> temptations, temperament, and character, as if told of another; and my father
> speaks openly of the ring to Mr. Forster—I do not mean to imply that the
> mystery itself had no strong hold on my father's imagination—[but] he was
> quite as deeply fascinated and absorbed in the study of the criminal Jasper,
> as in the dark and sinister crime that has given the book its title. And he also

speaks to Mr. Forster of the murder of a nephew by an uncle. He does not say that he is uncertain whether he shall save the nephew, but has evidently made up his mind that the crime is to be committed.

And at a later point:

If my father again changed his plan for the story of *Edwin Drood* the first thing he would naturally do would be to write to Mr. Forster and inform him of the alteration. We might imagine for an instant that he would perhaps desire to keep the change as a surprise for his friend, but—Mr. Forster's [jealous and exacting] character renders this supposition out of the question.— That he did not write to Mr. Forster to tell him of any divergence from his second plan for the book we all know, and we know also that my eldest brother Charles positively declared that he had heard from his father's lips that Edwin Drood was dead. Here, therefore, are two very important witnesses to a fact that is still doubted by those who never met my father, and were never impressed by the grave sincerity with which he would have given this assurance.

I shall let Charles Dickens the younger, the second witness mentioned by Mrs. Perugini, speak for himself. In the introduction which he wrote for an edition of *Edwin Drood* in 1931 he says:

It was during the last walk I ever had with him at Gadshill, and our talk, which had been principally concerned with literary matters connected with *All the Year Round,* presently drifting to *Edwin Drood,* my father asked me if I did not think that he had let out too much of his story too soon. I assented and added: "Of course, Edwin Drood was murdered?" Whereupon he turned upon me with an expression of astonishment at my having asked such an unnecessary question, and said: "Of course; what else did you suppose?"

As a final offering, I should like to bring forward the evidence of Sir Luke Fildes, able illustrator of the text of the novel. He first became acquainted with Charles Dickens when he was chosen to replace Charles Allston Collins, a brother of Wilkie Collins, and Kate Dickens's first husband. Charles Collins was the designer of the green cover for the monthly parts of *Edwin Drood*—the cover with the pictures that have been so controversial throughout the past seventy-odd years. He was to have illustrated the text as well, but failing health made the latter undertaking impossible. Sir Luke Fildes was therefore chosen to replace him, and his drawings proved wonderfully in harmony with the grim tone of the mystery.

J. W. T. Ley, in *The Dickens Circle,* tells us something of interest about the relationship existing between Charles Dickens and his illustrator, then a young man:

They had known one another for only a few months when the novelist was struck down. That sorrowful event occurred on a Wednesday evening. On the following morning Dickens was to have gone to London for the remainder of the week, and he was to have been accompanied on his return by the young artist, whose visit had been arranged so that he might become acquainted with the neighbourhood in which most of the scenes in the books [*sic*] were laid. We know that he was to have accompanied the novelist to Maidstone Gaol, there to see the condemned cell, with a view to a subsequent illustration.

Another sentence or two from Ley's book will serve to introduce the warm yet dignified letter written by Fildes, a letter which I consider invaluable in the light of the evidence it contains.

A few years ago Sir Luke Fildes gave expression to his regard for the novelist in an indignant letter he wrote to "The Times." A reviewer of Andrew Lang's book, "The Puzzle of Dickens's Last Plot," had suggested that the hints dropped by Dickens to Forster and to members of his family as to the plot, might have been intentionally misleading.

The letter itself, addressed to the Editor of *The Times*, follows.

Sir,—in an article entitled "The Mysteries of Edwin Drood," in your issue of to-day [October 27, 1905], the writer, speculating on the various theories advanced as solutions of the mystery, ventures to say:—

"Nor do we attach much importance to any of the hints Dickens dropped, whether to John Forster, to any member of his family, or to either of his illustrators. He was very anxious that his secret should not be guessed, and the hints which he dropped may very well have been intentionally misleading."

I know that Charles Dickens was very anxious that his secret should not be guessed, but it surprises me to read that he could be thought capable of the deceit so lightly attributed to him.

The "hints he dropped" to me, his sole illustrator—for Charles Collins, his son-in-law, only designed the green cover for the monthly parts, and Collins told me he did not in the least know the significance of the various groups in the design; that they were drawn from instructions personally given by Charles Dickens, and not from any text—these "hints" to me were the out-come of a request of mine that he would explain some matters, the meaning of which I could not comprehend, and which were for me, his illustrator, embarrassingly hidden.

I instanced in the printers' rough proof of the monthly part sent to me to illustrate where he particularly described John Jasper as wearing a neckerchief of such dimensions as to go twice round his neck. I called his attention to the circumstance that I had previously dressed Jasper as wearing a little black tie once round the neck, and I asked him if he had any special reasons for the alteration of Jasper's attire, and, if so, I submitted I ought to know. He, Dickens, appeared for the moment to be disconcerted by my remark, and said something meaning he was afraid he was "getting on too fast" and revealing more than he meant at that early stage, and after a short silence, cogitating, he suddenly said, "Can you keep a secret?" I assured him he could rely on me. He then said, "I must have the double necktie! It is necessary, for Jasper strangles Edwin Drood with it."

I was impressed by his earnestness, as indeed, I was at all my interviews with him—also by the confidence which he said he reposed in me, trusting that I would not in any way refer to it, as he feared even a chance remark might find its way into the papers "and thus anticipate his 'mystery' "; and it is a little startling, after more than thirty-five years of profound belief in the nobility of character and sincerity of Charles Dickens, to be told now that he probably was more or less of a humbug on such occasions.—I am, Sir, yours obediently.

                                                                LUKE FILDES
Harrogate, October 27.

Nowhere in the text of the novel as we have it today is there any description of John Jasper wearing a neckerchief "of such dimensions as to go twice round his neck." It is clear to me that the printers' rough proof was revised by Dickens, and that he substituted for the double necktie that great black silk scarf which Jasper hung in a loop upon his arm before he, too, went up the postern stair to greet his dinner guests. But there is no doubting the ring of utter sincerity in the letter Sir Luke Fildes wrote from his heart. Everything in the novel points to the fact that Edwin Drood was to meet death by strangulation at the hands of his uncle Jasper—that he was to be murdered.

Both Charles Dickens the younger and Sir Luke Fildes bear witness to the novelist's concern lest he had been getting on too fast and had let out too much of his story too soon. John Forster has written to the same effect, although he had in mind Dickens's anxiety about the early introduction of the Datchery assumption.

I do not think that the great novelist need have concerned himself in this way; his worry on these scores is to me a revelation of his ill health and of the approaching culmination of his dynamic life. Despite his fears, and even in its half-completed form, *The Mystery of Edwin Drood* has never been solved to the complete satisfaction of everyone. It remains an abiding mystery in a very real sense. There will be other books and articles written about it in the years to come; they will deal with new theories concerning the true identity of Dick Datchery, or the enigmatic nature of John Jasper, or all those foreshadowings of things to come that point in so tantalizing a manner to this or that conception of how Dickens might have developed the plot in the six parts never to appear before our eyes in print. But it is my firm belief that he played fair with his readers; that we may at least be certain of the death of Edwin Drood—certain that he was murdered by his uncle. Even with such assurance, mystery still remains. We have merely begun to unravel the strands that form only a part of the complicated texture; its final pattern we may never wholly reconstruct.

On January 7, 1914, there was heard by Justice Gilbert Keith Chesterton, sitting with a special jury in the King's Hall, Covent Garden, the trial of John Jasper, Lay Precentor of Cloisterham Cathedral in the County of Kent, for the murder of Edwin Drood, Engineer. I have read the verbatim report of this trial—a literary *tour de force* of varying degrees of interest—printed from the shorthand notes of J. W. T. Ley. It lasted almost five hours; no less a personage than Mr. Bernard Shaw was foreman of the jury; the verdict was manslaughter.

With that Shavian drollery for which he is so justly renowned, the distinguished playwright returned the verdict as follows:

My Lord,—I am happy to be able to announce to your Lordship that we, following the tradition and practice of British Juries, have arranged our verdict in the luncheon interval. I should explain, my Lord, that it undoubtedly presented itself to us as a point of extraordinary difficulty in this case, that a man should disappear absolutely and completely, having cut off all communication with his friends in Cloisterham; but having seen and heard the society and conversation of Cloisterham here in Court to-day, we no longer feel the slightest surprise at that. Now, under the influence of that observation, my Lord, the more extreme characters, if they will allow me to say so, in this Jury, were at first inclined to find a verdict of Not Guilty, because there was no evidence of a murder having been committed; but on the other hand, the calmer and more judicious spirits among us felt that to allow a man who had committed a cold-blooded murder of which his own nephew was the victim, to leave the dock absolutely unpunished, was a proceeding which would probably lead to our all being murdered in our beds. And so you will be glad to learn that the spirit of compromise has prevailed, and we find the prisoner guilty of Manslaughter.

We recommend him most earnestly to your Lordship's mercy, whilst at the same time begging your Lordship to remember that the protection of the lives of the community is in your hands, and begging you not to allow any sentimental consideration to deter you from applying the law in its utmost vigour.

Surely a most unaccountable verdict!

With it in mind, I should like to propose another—one which the reader of this study shall receive as judge. Let him suppose that John Jasper has again been on trial for his life, charged with murder in the first degree, willful and premeditated. The evidence of the novel itself to support the contention that Edwin Drood died as the result of a murderous assault committed upon his person by his uncle has been presented to the best of my ability. The testimony of various competent witnesses has been taken. The members of the jury are now returning to the courtroom to deliver their verdict. They file slowly into the box; the reader, as judge, looks at their faces and realizes that they are all either characters of fiction or actual personages long since departed from this life. This jury is composed of both men and women, and its panel reads as follows:

1) Hiram Grewgious, foreman; he has waived his right of exemption. Being a lawyer, he might well have declined to serve, but he is a man of absolute integrity, with a stern duty to perform.

2) Rosa Bud, soon to become Mrs. Tartar.

3) Helena Landless, pledged to Minor Canon Crisparkle.

4) Durdles, the stonemason, in a state of unhappy sobriety.

5) The Rev. Septimus Crisparkle. He, too, has waived his right of exemption.

6) Deputy, who feels gingerly of his neck as he looks at the defendant in the dock.

7) The Opium Woman, restraining with difficulty an impulse to shake her fists at the defendant.

8) Sir Luke Fildes, R.A.

9) Charles Dickens the younger.

10) Mrs. Perugini, formerly Kate Dickens.

11) John Forster, literary critic, author, and biographer.

12) Charles Dickens.

Surely an improbable jury! But with literary license, with complete disregard for strict practice and procedure, and with no concern for the fact that Rosa Bud and Deputy are minors, the twelve may be allowed to return their verdict. If I mistake not, the reader—as judge—will hear old Hiram Grewgious say in measured, deliberate tones: "Guilty, my Lord!"

What Might Have Been

(PART ONE)

H<small>IS GAZE</small> wandered from the windows to the stars, as if he would have read in them something that was hidden from him. Many of us would, if we could; but none of us so much as know our letters in the stars yet—or seem likely to do it, in this state of existence—and few languages can be read until their alphabets are mastered.

❖   ❖   ❖

These closing lines of chapter xvii in *The Mystery of Edwin Drood* are particularly fitting as an introduction to a study intended to deal largely with the unwritten half of Charles Dickens's last, un-finished work. Without too manifest a striving for effect, we may consider the twenty-three chapters of the fragment we have today as so many windows opening upon a perspective of nocturnal sky. That sky is speckled with stars, and those stars are the foreshadow-ings and incidents of the plot developed by Dickens through the first six monthly parts of his novel. Like old Hiram Grewgious, we fix our critical gaze upon those heavenly bodies; we seek to read in them much that was hidden from us when Dickens put down his pen for the last time on Wednesday, June 8, 1870. Only a few hours later he suffered the stroke that proved fatal and ended for-ever the activity of his vast creative genius. Ever since that day, men and women have sought to penetrate the mystery left by his death, to read the stars according to their varied abilities. I should like now to add another reading to the long and impressive list, but whether I have mastered the alphabet of the language of the stars that shine in the fragmentary firmament called *The Mystery of Edwin Drood* will be for the reader to judge.

What sort of novel have we to consider when we turn to the fragment that occupied the mind of the novelist during a good portion of the last two years of his life? Gilbert Chesterton, widely accepted as an authority on the works of Dickens, speaks about it thus in his critical study of the man: "His last book, *The Mystery of Edwin Drood,* depends entirely upon construction, even upon a centralized strategy. He staked everything upon a plot; he who had been the weakest of plotters, weaker than Sim Tappertit. He essayed a detective story, he who could never keep a secret; and he has kept it to this day. A new Dickens was really being born when Dickens died." George Santayana, who devoted one of his *Soliloquies in England and Later Soliloquies* to Dickens, states: "In his last book he was going to describe a love that was passionate and criminal." While the master of paradox and the eminent philospher are both correct in their appraisals, they might have gone a step farther. *Edwin Drood* is indeed a detective story with a complicated plot, and it does involve a love that is not only passionate but criminal. But in addition, as I have endeavored to make clear in previous studies, it paints the psychological portrait of a murderer with whom Charles Dickens identified himself. Here, as in all his previous writings, Dickens had something personal to say. What that was is to me one of the most interesting aspects of the mystery.

Some of those who have tried their hands at reading the stars have presented their findings in the form of sequels to the existing fragment. My own feeling about such continuations of *Edwin Drood* is that writers make a great mistake in attempting them. With all due respect for human ingenuity, I hold that no one can adequately carry on from where Dickens left off. Even though we consider our conclusions logical and inevitable, we still lack certainty; nor can we ever achieve more than a feeble imitation of that style so peculiarly his own.[1] A far more successful attempt to solve the mystery in fictional form was that employed by Dr. Austin Freeman, who wrote *The Mystery of Angelina Frood*. Here we find Dickens's basic plot transferred to entirely new surroundings, and developed with a fresh set of characters.

But we may speculate upon the forward movement of the novel in its unwritten portion, studying the foreshadowings and incidents already given us or considering certain landmarks that have been used time and time again in attempts to arrive at some satisfactory solution of the mystery. Having written at some length concerning the Datchery assumption; the nature and activities of John Jasper; the genesis of the novel; and the problem of whether or not Edwin Drood was murdered, I intend to review in this final study what I shall call the lesser landmarks. These are four, as I see them, and comprise the Sapsea fragment, the controversial green cover of the monthly parts, certain minor characters of the novel, and the use of hypnotism throughout the story.

A few years after the death of Dickens, his friend John Forster found among the sheets of one of the novelist's other manuscripts "some detached slips of his writing, on paper only half the size of that used for the tale, so cramped, interlined, and blotted as to be nearly illegible, which on close inspection proved to be a scene in which Sapsea the auctioneer is introduced as the principal figure, among a group of characters new to the story." This brief manuscript, entitled "How Mr. Sapsea ceased to be a member of the Eight Club. Told by himself," is generally known as the "Sapsea frag-

---

[1] Without any comment on the merits or faults of such individual conclusions as have come to my attention, I list them in chronological order, for the benefit of those readers who may be interested in them.

1. Orpheus C. Kerr [R. H. Newell], *The Cloven Foot*, 1870.
2. Henry Morford, *John Jasper's Secret*, 1871–1872.
3. *The Mystery of Edwin Drood*. Complete. *Part Second of the Mystery of Edwin Drood*, by the spirit-pen of Charles Dickens through a medium, 1873.
4. Gillan Vase [Mrs. Richard Newton], *A Great Mystery Solved*, 1878.
5. *The Mystery of Edwin Drood*. Completed in 1914 by W. E. C.
6. Dickens's *Mystery of Edwin Drood*. Completed by a Loyal Dickensian, 1927.
7. Edward Harris, *John Jasper's Gatehouse*, 1931.
8. Bruce Graeme, *Epilogue*, 1934.

ment." I do not believe that it helps us greatly to arrive at any sound conclusion concerning the plot development in the unwritten part of the novel.

I cannot accept Forster's explanation of the fragment: that Dickens, "having become a little nervous about the course of the tale, from a fear that he might have plunged too soon into the incidents leading on to the catastrophe, such as the Datchery assumption in the fifth number (a misgiving he had certainly expressed to his sister-in-law)," had decided to "open some fresh veins of character incidental to the interest, though not directly part of it, and so to handle them in connection with Sapsea as a little to suspend the final development even while assisting to strengthen it." To my mind, this fragment represents no more than a step taken by Dickens in the building up of Sapsea's character. Told in the first person, it could hardly have been introduced into the narrative of *Edwin Drood*, since the novel is written from the author's omnipresent point of view. But as a revealing study of the pompous Mayor of Cloisterham, it is a little gem. Here is the solemn ass in all his glory, with his delusion that he knew the world, his passion for emulating the Dean, and his conceited belief that he was capable of handling men. I have no doubt that Dickens used this study when he came to the actual writing of *Edwin Drood*, but I look upon it as merely preliminary material for the novel.

Nor do I believe that Poker, the young man who professed to find in Sapsea a personage high in the Church, was an early model for Dick Datchery. This Poker flatters the auctioneer to the top of his bent, as does Datchery, and even asserts that he came to the town (unnamed in the fragment) for the sole purpose of seeing and hearing him. But Datchery flatters him in a more subtle manner, and for a definite purpose: the gleaning of information. The idea that Poker served as a model for Datchery may have arisen from the fact that the young man is represented as speaking to Sapsea by the churchyard, where Datchery converses with His Honor in one of the novel's choicest scenes. Beyond that coincidence, however, there is no similarity between the two men. No; I can see in this brief fragment nothing more than a trial sketch for what was later to become a more finished portrait.

The bluish green cover for the monthly instalments of *Edwin Drood* presents perhaps the most controversial of all the subjects relating to the novel; mentioned sooner or later by practically everyone who has written about *Edwin Drood*, it has become something of a mystery in its own right. Presumably it was designed by Charles Allston Collins, Dickens's son-in-law, for on September 24, 1869, the novelist wrote to Frederic Chapman, his publisher, as follows: "Charles Collins wishes to try his hand at illustrating my new book. I want him to try the cover first. Please send down to him at Gad's Hill, any of our old green covers that you may have by you." And Dickens later wrote, at the end of a letter quoted by Forster: "Charles Collins has designed an excellent cover."

In spite of this evidence, *The Sphere,* in the issue of February 9, 1929, published an article by Walter Dexter, editor of *The Dickensian,* entitled "New Light on *Edwin Drood,*" wherein Dexter stated that new discoveries concerning the cover "were made in the autumn of 1926, when Professor C. F. Lehmann-Haupt was on a visit to Sir Henry and Lady Dickens. It was then that Lady Dickens (to whom the professor is distantly related) told him that the final drawing was done by Luke Fildes." The original design by Collins—in an unfinished state—was reproduced as an illustration for this article; it is interesting to note that Collins sketched in place of the three men on the winding staircase—men with whose appearance every student of the novel is probably familiar—three helmeted gentlemen equipped with truncheons and handcuffs; in other words, the police. And in "New Facts Concerning *Edwin Drood*" (*The Dickensian,* 1929) Professor Lehmann-Haupt writes: "Before I made this important fact public, I wrote to Lady Dickens asking her kindly to confirm it, which she did, saying: 'I *did* tell you that Charles Collins made the first drawing for the cover of *Edwin Drood,* but he fell ill and did not finish it. Luke Fildes con-

tinued and finished the drawing with several alterations.' " That
is all I have been able to discover in connection with the origin of
the green cover; and since Sir Luke Fildes died in 1927, it is unlikely that he expressed any opinion on the statements made by
Professor Lehmann–Haupt.

When we contemplate the cover itself and ask the question, What
clue or clues does it afford to the story as it might logically have
been developed? we fall into the realm of mere conjecture. On its
dexter side, attached to the meager wreath encircling the title: "The
Mystery of Edwin Drood. / by Charles Dickens. / with illustrations," we find a few roses, some in the bud and some in full bloom.
Here, I take it, is the symbolic presentation of the feminine influence in the story; the love interest. In the upper right-hand corner,
a female figure suggestive of happiness holds a flower above her
head. The sinister side of the encircling wreath bears nothing but
thorns, suggestive of the male element, and perhaps a motif of
murder. An avenging fury with snakelike hair—or possibly a figure
emblematical of tragedy,—dagger in hand, matches the happy creature on the right, and dominates the upper left-hand corner. Extending between these two figures and occupying almost the entire
upper third of the cover is a scene depicting Rosa and Edwin leaving the cathedral. Rosa's face is turned away from young Drood,
who looks straight ahead; neither of them has a happy expression.
They are on the dexter side of the vignette, and typify the "boy
and girl going apart from one another." On the sinister side stands
Jasper, right hand to mouth, gazing at the young couple. Two
ecclesiastical gentlemen, preceded by an equal number of choir
boys, are on Jasper's left. The scene is certainly not in the novel,
although in his "Number Plans" for the fourth monthly part Dickens wrote: "Last meeting of Rosa & Edwin in ["in" crossed out,
caret inserted, and "outside" written above] the Cathedral? *Yes.*"

Below this scene, on the dexter side, are three vignettes descend-
ing perpendicularly to the bottom of the cover. The uppermost of
the three reveals a girl or young woman, with long hair down her

back, looking intently at a placard or bill whereon is visible the word "LOST." The features of this unknown person are not discernible, but she appears to be youthful. It has been argued that the figure represents Rosa, fleeing from Jasper to her guardian in London and stopping to look at one of the posters that Jasper caused to be circulated shortly after Edwin's disappearance. That the poster has been up for some time is inferable from its downward-curling corner. I have said that this woman appears to be youthful, but sometimes I am not so certain of her age; sometimes I am inclined to believe that she may be the Opium Woman, for reasons to be given later in more detail. Certainly I am convinced that the Opium Woman saw such placards in London and made use of the knowledge gained therefrom.

The next vignette, immediately below the woman facing the poster, depicts a young lady seated on a rustic bench. A man, kneeling at her right, is kissing her hand. This man bears no resemblance to the Jasper of the Cathedral scene, but despite that fact I feel sure that this picture refers to the melodramatic interview between Rosa and Jasper by the sundial in the garden of the Nuns' House. Certainly Sir Luke Fildes used a similar type of bench in his text illustration of that moving encounter. Some interpreters of the cover have read into this picture a proposal on the part of Tartar. Mr. Percy Carden avers that the kneeling man is Neville Landless avowing his love to Rosa, because he has a mustache, and because Miss Ferdinand, a pupil at Miss Twinkleton's, "got into new trouble by surreptitiously clapping on a paper moustache at dinner-time, and going through the motions of aiming a water-bottle at Miss Giggles, who drew a table-spoon in defense." This episode took place on the day following the quarrel between Neville Landless and Edwin Drood in Jasper's rooms. Inasmuch as Miss Ferdinand was playing the part of young Landless, Mr. Carden infers that he must have worn a mustache, and so the man in the picture is Neville. I have never been able to read into Miss Ferdinand's action more than a schoolgirl's natural way of playing the part of a male, especially of a male whom she supposes to be a villain. Nor am I perturbed by the fact that the man and woman in the garden scene are not dressed in mourning, as were Rosa and Jasper in the novel. When the cover was designed, Charles Dickens could not have had in mind every last minute detail of the story. And so I have no hesitation in accepting this sketch as the scene by the sundial.

The drawing at the very bottom of the dexter side shows the Opium Woman sitting on her bedstead, pipe in hand, and holding the container from which she takes her "mixter"—although this container is far too large to be a "thimble."

The sinister side of the cover has what appears at first glance to be three sketches to match the ones I have just discussed, and these I shall consider in ascending order. Right at the bottom is John Chinaman, a logcial counterpart of the Princess Puffer. Above him two men are climbing a winding staircase, presumably in the cathedral tower. Above them again is a third man, mounting two steps at a time, bending over the railing and pointing upward with his right hand. Much has been made of the fact that he points straight at Jasper in the cathedral scene. Since these three climbers replace the policemen in the original sketch made by Charles Collins, I infer that they are all going up the staircase at the same time; that we should consider them part of a single drawing; and that we are not dealing with separate ascents at odd intervals. I have always considered this scene to represent the pursuit of Jasper, destined to reach its climax on the summit of the cathedral tower. The topmost climber I take to be Tartar. The next individual, who is likewise going up two steps at a time, I take to be Datchery. His face is so obscured by the stone pivot of the stairs that it is little more than a blur, but he is tall and angular. The man lowest down on the stairs looks back with a mournful expression; he, too, points upward, but with far less vehemence in his gesture than that displayed by the topmost climber. I believe him to be Neville. Since no one of the three wears ecclesiastical dress, I presume that Minor Canon Crisparkle is not visible, although on his way up the staircase.

Within the circle of roses and thorns just below the caption "with illustrations" are a crossed key and spade, forming an arch above what is clearly Durdles's dinner bundle. The bundle, by association, leads me to identify the key as that of the Sapsea tomb. The spade immediately suggests the digging of graves, or the removal of quick-lime from the mound in Durdles's yard.

I have saved for final consideration the sketch at the bottom of the cover, a pendant to the cathedral scene above. This is the most controversial picture of all. A man holding a lantern in his right hand is entering some sort of room; he has pushed open a door, which has swung back to his left, and he seems to have his left hand on the knob. Before him stands a youth dressed in a long paletot and wearing a broad-brimmed hat. This young man's left hand is holding the flap of his coat; he is not thrusting his hand inside the coat, as some have assumed.

The man with the lantern has invariably been taken to be John Jasper. I do not demur. I am equally certain that the young man facing Jasper is neither Neville Landless nor his sister Helena in the guise of Dick Datchery. Since he closely resembles the youth in the cathedral scene, I assume him to be Edwin Drood.

But I do not for one moment believe, as did Richard Proctor and others, that this sketch represents a tomb, or that Edwin Drood is confronting his wicked uncle who has come into the burial place of his nephew to seek the ring of diamonds and rubies, as I am convinced he ultimately did. The room or chamber—whatever it may be called—is too large for a tomb, and there is no trace of either coffin or sarcophagus. Furthermore the door has a rim lock, of a type not usually found in the entrances to tombs, and I can detect evidence to indicate that it is paneled. It swings inward and to the left, as would a door opening out of a hallway. Besides, if I were John Jasper, and were entering the tomb wherein I had concealed the body of the nephew I had murdered, I certainly would not do so with a *lighted* lantern in my hand. I should wait until the door were tightly closed; then and only then would I light the lantern.

No; this "place" is not a tomb. I have always felt it to be a room in the gatehouse, and the vignette itself to be indicative of an event that took place on the night of Edwin Drood's murder. Let me reconstruct the scene. The dinner given by Jasper to young Landless and his nephew on that momentous Christmas Eve has been over for some hours; the youths have shaken hands and patched up their quarrel, and the time has passed pleasantly enough. But the "storms of wind" mentioned by Dickens in his "plans" have arisen; the two young men go down to the river to watch the action of this tempest. We learn from the story that they did not spend more than ten minutes at the water's edge. But how long did it take them to get there? And how much time did Edwin Drood take in returning to the gatehouse after he had left Neville at Mr. Crisparkle's door?

Is it not conceivable that Jasper, in the overwrought state of mind that must have been his on the very night when he had planned to murder Edwin, could not await calmly his nephew's return, but set forth to meet him, lantern in hand? And is it not equally possible that Edwin came back to the gatehouse without having encountered his uncle, and arrived there before him? Such, at least, is my contention.

In *The Dickensian* for 1929 there is an article by H. W. Jamieson and F. M. B. Rosenthal, entitled, "The Mystery of Edwin Drood—Some New Keys that Fit." These writers likewise refuse to accept the theory that the Jasper of the much-disputed vignette is entering a tomb, and offer an explanation not only highly original in nature but based upon their own personal investigation as well.

"In Rochester Cathedral itself [they write] . . . there is a door which exactly tallies with the door in the picture—a high, massive door with a rim lock, that opens outwards from right to left as one comes from the side on which the lock is fixed. This door is in the South Choir aisle and opens on a short flight of steps, at the foot of which lies the passage at the side of the chancel into which Jasper and Durdles emerged from the crypt on the night of the unaccountable expedition." And further on they state: "The lamp is another very important point in favour of this being the spot indicated in the picture. It is not the type of lamp a man would carry about with him, but it is exactly the type that would be found in the Cathedral."

I should like to add in passing that it pleased me to find that these writers consider Grewgious to be Datchery, and that they venture the opinion that quicklime may have *preserved* Drood's body. Since I had arrived at the same conclusion with regard to the old lawyer long before I read their article, my pleasure will be readily understood. And their suggestion that quicklime might preserve a body led me to obtain the scientific confirmation of that fact introduced in my study, "Was Edwin Drood Murdered?"

But to return to the cover. The reader must have gathered by this time that very little can be deduced from it to elucidate the future plot development of the novel. Such is indeed the case. All that I have said—and I could have gone on at far greater length—shows that the collection of sketches served its purpose well: the cover did undoubtedly attract attention and arouse interest in the minds of Dickens's readers even before they realized that the story they were following from month to month would never reach completion. But I honestly doubt that it did much more. And so it is logical to conclude that Charles Dickens was purposely vague in his instructions to Collins and to Sir Luke Fildes, and that he would hardly have given away the heart of his mystery in what was actually of no more significance than our dust jackets today.

When we take up the minor characters of the novel, we find a far more fertile field for our conjectures concerning the probable development of plot. The Opium Woman, Deputy, Bazzard, and Luke Honeythunder all had more or less important parts to play; but of these four the Opium Woman looms largest.

Despite her infrequent appearances—she is to be found only in chapters i, xiv, and xxiii of the novel's printed version—the Opium Woman is a most consistently drawn character, and one who was destined to exert a definite influence on the course of the story. To

be sure, Dickens originally intended to have her make a brief entrance into the chapter entitled "Mr. Durdles and Friend." That
purpose is evidenced by his "plans" for this particular section of
the novel, for we read: "Carry through the woman of the 1st Chapter." The injunction is underlined, but beyond it, on the left-hand
side of the sheet, we discover an emphatic: "*No.*" Now "Mr. Durdles and Friend" was to have been chapter viii of Part II; but when
Dickens learned in December, 1869, that his first two numbers
were, together, twelve printed pages too short, he transposed this
chapter from Number II to Number I, where it became chapter v,
and was obliged to remodel Number II. His original manuscript
contains a scene near the end of "Mr. Durdles and Friend" wherein
Jasper and the stonemason overhear the Opium Woman talking
to Deputy just outside the door of the Travellers' Twopenny.

The keynote of the Opium Woman's character is her desire for
money, so clearly shown in her encounters with John Jasper, Edwin
Drood, and Dick Datchery. In the marvelous opening chapter of
the story, she says to John Jasper: "Ye'll remember like a good soul,
won't ye, that the market price [of opium] is dreffle high just now?
More nor three shillings and sixpence for a thimbleful!—Ye'll pay
me accordingly, deary, won't ye?" Of Edwin Drood, on the eve of
the fateful dinner at the gatehouse, with his uncle and young Landless, she makes a forthright demand: "Look'ee, deary; give me
three-and-sixpence, and don't you be afeard for me." And later: "If
you don't give me three-and-sixpence, don't give me a brass farden.
And if you do give me three-and-sixpence, deary, I'll tell you something." When she is walking with Datchery through the streets of
Cloisterham shortly after her first meeting him, she asks: "Wouldn't
you help me to pay for my traveller's lodging, dear gentleman, and
to pay my way along? I am a poor soul, I am indeed, and troubled
with a grievous cough."

There is method in Dickens's emphasis on this urge for money,
the old crone's outstanding characteristic. Just as in his reiteration
of her tendency to self-pity, which goes hand in hand with her

desire for gold. "O me, O me, my lungs is weak, my lungs is bad!—
Ah, poor me, poor me, my poor hand shakes like to drop off!" is
her refrain to Jasper. "My lungs is weakly; my lungs is dreffle bad.
Poor me, poor me, my cough is rattling dry!" Thus she seeks to
play upon the sympathy of young Drood. With Datchery she is
less insistent upon her infirmities; she seems to recognize the fact
that the white-haired stranger is not the man to be taken in. But
as we have seen, she does work in her lament, "I am a poor soul, I
am indeed, and troubled with a grievous cough."

Now so strong an urge for money—spent beyond a doubt in the
purchase of opium,—especially when linked with the self-pity she
feels as the result of her wretched condition, constitutes a pregnant
incentive to blackmail. And here, I believe, is the reason why she
comes to Cloisterham for the first time in search of Jasper. The
opening chapter is purposely vague as to time, but Dickens does
tell us: "Not only is the day waning, but the year.—There has been
rain this afternoon, and a wintry shudder goes among the little
pools on the cracked, uneven flagstones . . . " Certainly it is late
autumn as the story opens. When the Opium Woman makes her
first visit to the cathedral town in quest of Jasper, it is shortly before
December 24, the day she encounters Edwin Drood. Now Jasper
has not been to her squalid den, so far as we can ascertain, since
the occasion of his debauch described with some detail in the opening chapter. Is it not conceivable that she has come to dun him for
money?

We do know that the choirmaster has been smoking opium on
his own, as the following passages disclose.

1. "He takes from a locked press a peculiar-looking pipe, which
he fills—but not with tobacco—and, having adjusted the contents
of the bowl, very carefully, with a little instrument, ascends an
inner staircase . . . " Chapter v.

2. " 'One would think, Jasper, you had been trying a new medicine for that occasional indisposition of yours.'

" 'No, really? That's well observed; for I have.' " Chapter xiv.

But while it is true that Jasper has smoked opium in the privacy of his chambers, thus depriving the old crone of trade, there is nothing to indicate that he has done so on or shortly before December 24. Andrew Lang is therefore making a gratuitous assumption when he says, in "The Puzzle of Dickens's Last Plot" (p. 25): "Please remark that Jasper has run up to town, on December 23, and has saturated his system with a debauch of opium on the very eve of the day when he clearly means to kill Edwin. This was a most injudicious indulgence, in the circumstances. A maiden murder needs nerve! We know that 'fiddlestrings was weakness to express the state of' Jasper's 'nerves' on the day after the night of opium with which the story opens. On December 24, Jasper returned home, the hag at his heels." Lang has no sound basis for making such an assertion; even the Minor Canon refers to Jasper's calm state on December 24.

I suppose Lang was led into this error by a speech made by the Opium Woman much later in the story. When she embarks upon her second pursuit of Jasper, in the closing chapter of the fragment, she says: "I'll not miss ye twice! I lost ye last, where that omnibus you got into nigh your journey's end plied betwixt the station and the place [Cloisterham]. I wasn't so much as certain that you even went right on to the place. Now I know ye did." But the Opium Woman here refers to a visit made by Jasper prior to December 24; she refers—if she has told the truth about the number of times she has been in Cloisterham—to that Monday night when she was seen at the Travellers' Twopenny by Jasper and Durdles, while the former was on his way home after the quarrel between his nephew and young Landless, and his subsequent visit to the house of Minor Canon Crisparkle. In other words, we must conclude that the Opium Woman remained in Cloisterham for some little time, almost a fortnight, since the famous quarrel occurred, in all probability, on Monday, December 12. After Dickens decided to remove the old hag from chapter viii, which was to become chapter v when he was obliged to transpose it from Part II to Part I because of the shortage in printed pages, he may have overlooked or forgotten the time elements involved, and may have proceeded later on the assumption that the Opium Woman actually had appeared in Cloisterham on the night of the quarrel. Whatever uncertainty arises in this question about when the woman arrived in Cloisterham for the first time is due, I believe, to that unfortunate transposition of a chapter.

At any rate, I am convinced that the Opium Woman must have been in Cloisterham prior to December 24, and that she had seen Rosa and Edwin together, and even overheard some of their conversation. Such a conviction is inevitable if one studies carefully what she says when she is found by Edwin on that particular date. It will be remembered that the young couple walked in the neighborhood of the cathedral and the river on Friday, December 23, for Edwin says to Rosa: "I dine with the dear fellow [his uncle] tomorrow and next day—Christmas Eve and Christmas Day." They sat upon some ruins, and strolled by the riverside, where they remained until after sunset. Then they came at last to the elm trees by the cathedral, and said their farewells, and there John Jasper saw their parting kiss.

On the next day—December 24—Edwin meets the Opium Woman at dusk in the Monks' Vineyard. And what does she say to him? She announces that she has come from London. "I came here, looking for a needle in a haystack [meaning Jasper], and I ain't found it." She informs him that she smokes opium; that if he will give her money, she will tell him something. When he does give her some, she says: "Bless ye! Hark'ee, dear genl'mn. What's your Chris'en name?" Why should she put a leading question like that if she had never seen him before? And mark what follows. He gives her his name, whereupon she murmurs: "Edwin, Edwin, Edwin. Is the short of that name Eddy?"

Now here is conclusive evidence that the old hag *has* seen and overheard the couple on the preceding day, for Dickens has told us that no one but Rosa ever calls young Drood "Eddy." This con-

clusion is strengthened by her very next speech, after Edwin has
replied in the affirmative: "Don't sweethearts call it so?" Can there
be any further doubt that she has seen Edwin with Rosa?

"How should I know?" is Edwin's answer to her last question.

"Haven't you a sweetheart, upon your soul?" she counters.

"None."

She turns away, but Edwin reminds her that she was to tell him
something.

"So I was, so I was," is her rejoinder. "Well, then. You be thank-
ful that your name ain't Ned."

Since this is Jasper's habitual nickname for his nephew, the inference that the Opium Woman has heard Jasper mention it in
wild talk during his debauches at her den leaps to the mind. She
is beginning to associate Jasper with the young man standing
before her through the media of "Edwin," "Eddy," and "Ned."

"Why?" asks Edwin.

"Because it's a bad name to have just now."

"How a bad name?"

"A threatened name. A dangerous name."

Jasper *has* talked in his opium-induced dreams; no other conclusion is tenable.

"The proverb says that threatened men live long," is Drood's
reply.

"Then Ned—so threatened is he, wherever he may be while I
am a-talking to you, deary [note the subtle way in which the
woman states indirectly her knowledge that young Drood *is* Ned],
should live to all eternity!"

And so Dickens drops another red herring to counteract such suspicions as may have been aroused in the reader's mind.

Like the three Weird Sisters who were weaving the fates of
Macbeth and Banquo in Shakespeare's great tragedy, the Opium
Woman plays her part in the respective destinies of John Jasper
and his nephew. She has warned Edwin of the danger overshadow-
ing him because he has satisfied her greed for money. The next

move is up to him. But we are told that he resolves to say nothing of all this to his uncle on that night.

It should be noted at this point in the novel that the old crone does not know Jasper's name, his calling, or even the fact that he is a resident of Cloisterham. That is evident from what she says in chapter xxiii: "I wasn't so much as certain that you even went right on to the place." But she must have had a dawning realization of a close tie of some sort between the man who came to her den to smoke opium and the youth she now knows as "Edwin."

When she makes her third appearance in the den with Jasper, she has become more subtle in her dealings with the choirmaster. I have no doubt that her chance meeting with Edwin has occupied her thoughts on more than one occasion; that she has turned over in her mind ways and means to capitalize on her meager information. I am equally certain that she has seen copies of the placard distributed in London through Jasper's efforts. Now although Dickens does not say this in so many words, it is reasonable to infer that Edwin's *full name* appeared on that placard; I am therefore convinced that the old crone knows by now who the lost youth really is.

After lighting her candle, she recognizes her visitor, who has not been to see her for some time.

"I didn't suppose you could have kept away, alive, so long," she says, "from the poor old soul with the real receipt for mixing it. And you are in mourning, too! Why didn't you come and have a pipe or two of comfort? Did they leave you money, perhaps, and so you didn't want comfort?"

Always the question of money! And we should note that it is not Jasper's mourning attire alone that prompts the old hag to take for granted the death of some person close to the choirmaster.

"Who was they as died, deary?"

She is beginning to pump Jasper; her mind goes back to Edwin to what she has read on the placards.

"A relative," he replies shortly.

"Died of what, lovey?"

"Probably, Death," is the curt answer.

She seeks to placate her visitor, who prepares himself for the opium pipe.

"Now you begin to look like yourself," she says. "Now I begin to know my old customer indeed!"

There is a double meaning in her last statement, for she has come to believe that Edwin's disappearance has the smell of murder about it, and that his murderer lies before her. And when she says, with reference to her wares, "He's going to take it in an artful form now, my deary dear!" she means that the "mixter" has been weakened by intent, so that she may get the smoker to talk. I have no doubt that she had long been planning for just such an opportunity.

It finally dawns on Jasper that the mixture is less potent than before. When he says as much, she is quick to reply: "It's just the same. Always the identical same." But we may be certain it is not.

As Jasper goes through what amounts to a confession of the murder of his nephew, the old crone is at his side, prompting him to continue, trying to pump him, like some evil bird of prey determined to tear his secret from his breast. And when at last he succumbs even to the weaker mixture of the drug and sinks into a stupor, she tries in vain to rouse him and flicks his face with the back of her hand.

"I heard ye say once, I heard ye say once, when I was lying where you're lying, and you were making your speculations upon me, 'Unintelligible!' I heard you say so, of two more than me. But don't ye be too sure always; don't ye be too sure, beauty!"

Jasper's wild words have been full of meaning—for her.

And presently she adds: "Not so potent as it once was? Ah! perhaps not at first. You may be more right there. Practice makes perfect. I may have learned the secret how to make ye talk, deary."

She might well have quoted another proverb: "A bird in the hand is worth two in the bush." I do not see how Dickens could have made it clearer that from then on she intends to blackmail Jasper.

When he leaves the den, she puts her plan into immediate execution, following him to his mean hotel in the back of Aldersgate Street. As soon as he has come out again, she follows him for a short distance, then enters the hotel herself.

"Is the gentleman from Cloisterham indoors?"

She knows now, beyond a shadow of a doubt, that he *is* from the cathedral town.

"Just gone out."

"Unlucky. When does the gentleman return to Cloisterham?"

"At six this evening."

She thanks her informant and hurries out. And then comes the gloating speech that proves her determination to blackmail the man who has been her best customer.

"I'll not miss ye twice! I lost ye last, where that omnibus you got into nigh your journey's end plied betwixt the station and the place. I wasn't so much as certain that you even went right on to the place. Now I know ye did. My gentleman from Cloisterham, I'll be there before ye, and bide your coming. I've swore my oath that I'll not miss ye twice!"

And so the harpy begins to close in on her prey.

I have never been persuaded that the Opium Woman is anything more than John Jasper's evil genius, a sordid creature who has made the most of an available opportunity. The greed for money so strongly implanted in her by Dickens has led to an inevitable conclusion: blackmail. That the old crone is related to Jasper by any tie of blood seems to me to be utter nonsense. So when J. Cuming Walters makes a statement to that effect, I cannot let it pass unchallenged. In *Clues to Dickens's Mystery of Edwin Drood,* he says of Jasper: "If we deduce that his father was an adventurer and a vagabond, we shall not be far wrong. If we deduce that his mother was the opium eater, prematurely aged, who had transmitted her vicious propensity to her child, we shall most certainly be right."

To this I say, "Nonsense!" We know that Jasper was some "six-and-twenty" years old when the story opens. We know further that the Opium Woman says of herself: "I got Heavens-hard drunk for sixteen year afore I took to this [opium]; but this don't hurt me, not to speak of." What we do not know is how long she has been engaged in the traffic of the drug. But despite this lack of knowledge—and despite the fact that we are not told her real age,—how can Walters argue that she is John Jasper's mother who transmitted a vicious propensity for opium to her son *after* he was born? From what he has said before, he does not use the term "transmitted" merely as a synonym for "handed on," without any implication that Jasper's addiction to the drug was a matter of inheritance. He deduces that the addiction *was* inherited. His deduction simply does not square with the facts in the case. If what he says were so— and it is not,—then the Opium Woman must have known that Jasper was her son. Now we shall see that when the old crone meets Datchery she has no inkling whatever of Jasper's name, profession, or even his place of residence in Cloisterham.

Walters offers a second theory—and to my mind this fact implies that even he entertained some doubt about his first; it also involves a close tie between the Opium Woman and Jasper. "Another hypothesis—following on the Carker theme in *Dombey and Son*—is that Jasper, a dissolute and degenerate man, lascivious, and heartless, may have wronged a child of the woman's; but it is not likely that Dickens would repeat the Mrs. Brown story." This concept leaves me as cold as the former, but I do agree that Dickens would hardly repeat the Mrs. Brown story. It strikes me that Walters has curiously misunderstood the nature of John Jasper. The man is a drug addict, to be sure, but he is neither dissolute nor degenerate. Lascivious, yes; so far as his passion for Rosa is of a lustful kind. Heartless, yes; for he killed the nephew whom he once loved—just as Dickens destroyed his family life when he forced a deed of separation on his wife and followed the urge of his infatuation for a young actress.

But let us observe the Opium Woman in her association with Dick Datchery. Soon after she meets the detecting personality of the novel, she learns Jasper's full name and where he lives. She likewise obtains the information that he sings in the cathedral choir. None of these facts had she possessed before. We may be sure of that when Dickens writes: "The burst of triumph in which she thanks him does not escape the notice of the single buffer of an easy temper living idly on his means. He glances at her; clasps his hands behind him, as the wont of such buffers is; and lounges along the echoing Precincts at her side." Her manifest glee at learning what she had never known before makes Dick Datchery want to know more about her and her interest in Jasper.

He suggests that she may go up at once to Mr. Jasper's rooms. She shakes her head, as "she eyes him with a cunning smile."

"O! you don't want to speak to him?"

She shakes her head again "and forms with her lips a soundless 'No.'" She is not to be rushed into a meeting with Jasper; she wants time to gloat over her new-found information and to lay her plans with care.

Mr. Datchery seeks to learn from whence she comes, but she evades his artfully framed question. He sees through her greedy nature, however, and his rattling of loose coins in his trousers' pockets brings forth the inevitable request for money, followed by the statement that she has been in Cloisterham only once before in all her life.

Pure chance has brought them to the Monks' Vineyard, where the surroundings—plus the still rattling coins—prompt her to recollect her interview with Edwin.

"By this token, though you mayn't believe it," she says. "That a young gentleman gave me three-and-sixpence as I was coughing my breath away on this very grass. I asked him for three-and-sixpence, and he gave it me."

She hopes Mr. Datchery will take the hint.

When that gentleman merely suggests that it was a little cool on her part to name her sum, she hurries into an explanation of why she wanted the money. She confesses that she wants opium; she states that it was last Christmas Eve that the young gentleman gave her money. She goes so far as to reveal the young gentleman's name: Edwin.

I am always impressed by the artistry with which Dickens handles this scene. The Opium Woman has given Datchery invaluable information simply because she craves the means of buying her favorite drug. She is acting throughout in character. At the same time, what the old crone does and says gives a new twist to the plot development of the story, since it paves the way for the subsequent use Dick Datchery will make of her.

"How do you know the young gentleman's name?" he asks.

"I asked him for it, and he told it me. I only asked him the two questions, what was his Chris'en name, and whether he'd a sweetheart? And he answered, Edwin, and he hadn't."

He gives her some money, and "with many servile thanks she goes her way."

But just as she is weaving her plans to blackmail Jasper, who has delivered himself into her hands, so she will be henceforth a pawn in the game whose moves are directed by Dick Datchery. When he sees her in the cathedral on the following morning—he has learned from Deputy that she plans to go there,—he is watching for her reaction to Jasper's appearance. He does not have to wait long to find out what it is. While Jasper chants and sings, she "shakes her fist at him behind the pillar's friendly shelter." And again: "she hugs herself in her lean arms, and then shakes both fists at the leader of the Choir."

To her simple mind, a man occupying so exalted a position—for such Jasper's office must seem to her—is a far riper subject for blackmail than she had anticipated. She cannot possibly restrain her unholy glee. Her actions do not escape the notice of Dick Datchery.

He speaks to her outside the cathedral.

"Well, mistress. Good morning. You have seen him?"

Still enraptured with her additional knowledge, she exclaims: "*I*'ve seen him, deary; *I*'ve seen him!"

"And you know him?"

"Know him! Better far than all the Reverend Parsons put together know him!"

And indeed she does, for she is convinced that he has murdered his nephew; she is convinced that she holds in her power a rich prize: a man who will pay as much as she may demand to keep safe his horrid secret and maintain his position in the Church. It is the realization of what has gone through her mind that leads Dick Datchery to perform a certain action before starting in upon his breakfast, prepared by Mrs. Tope.

"Before sitting down to it, he opens his corner-cupboard door; takes his bit of chalk from its shelf; adds one thick line to the score, extending from the top of the cupboard door to the bottom; and then falls to with an appetite."

Those were the last words of his novel Charles Dickens was ever to write, but in setting them down he informed his readers that Dick Datchery considered the Opium Woman the most valuable agent he could employ in the tracking down of John Jasper.

What Might Have Been

(Part Two)

T HE IMPISH DEPUTY, a "hideous small boy" of uncertain age, was likewise to play a part of some importance in *The Mystery of Edwin Drood,* although he appears in only four chapters of the existing fragment. Dickens has drawn him with the same care he expended on the Opium Woman, and the nameless waif moves us in much the same way as Gavroche, the *gamin* of *Les Misérables.*

I have called him nameless, for "Deputy" is no more than a term indicative of his lowly occupation at the Travellers' Twopenny. In a contribution to *Household Words,* published June 14, 1851, "On Duty with Inspector Field," Dickens wrote: "Why Deputy, Inspector Field can't say. He only knows that the man who takes care of the beds and lodgers is always called so." "Deputy" is likewise a synonym for "agent," so we shall not be surprised to find that this tatterdemalion is to become an assistant of Dick Datchery's, and that he, too, is to be instrumental in bringing John Jasper to justice.

When we first meet him in the chapter entitled "Mr. Durdles and Friend," we are conscious of his almost instinctive hatred of the choirmaster. Being such a small lad, he talks big to make up for his diminutive stature; but there is no mistaking the antipathy underlying the very first words he hurls at Jasper in lieu of the stones clutched in his hands: "Yes, I'll give 'em you down your throat, if you come a-ketching hold of me. I'll smash your eye, if you don't look out!"

An intense individualist, Deputy reverses the normal order of procedure in society through his quaint task of stoning Durdles home: the child looks after the man. And just as religion and the law are to be arrayed against John Jasper in the persons of Minor Canon Crisparkle and Hiram Grewgious, so the lowest rank of the social hierarchy will work against him in Deputy, one of its most humble representatives.

In "A Night with Durdles," this lad's hatred of Jasper is again manifest; once more emphasis is laid on the choirmaster's eye, almost as if Deputy sensed the hypnotic power possessed by Jasper. "I'll blind yer, s'elp me!" cries Deputy. "I'll stone yer eyes out, s'elp me! If I don't have yer eyesight, bellows me!" I shall have more to say about John Jasper's mesmeric abilities later on; it is worth noting that they are apparent even to this boy.

Dickens's memorandum for his manuscript "Plans" concerning Deputy's appearance in this chapter is not without its significance for the future development of the plot. "Keep the boy suspended," is what he wrote. There is no doubt that Deputy has seen Jasper at work after the "unaccountable expedition" has culminated in Durdles's drugged dream. When the boy cries out to Jasper, who accuses him of eavesdropping: "Yer lie, I haven't. I'd only jist come out for my 'elth when I see you two a-coming out of the Kinfreederel," we know that he is lying. Just as he lies in a more humorous vein in chapter xviii, when Datchery comes upon him stoning a sheep and accuses him of laming it. "Yer lie," is the lad's instant retort. "'E went and lamed isself. I see 'im do it, and I giv' 'im a shy as a Widdy-warning to 'im not to go a-bruisin' 'is master's mutton any more."

The boy's friendly relation with Datchery is based upon his realization that the white-haired stranger is no friend of Jasper's, and upon an intuitive feeling that Datchery is out to track down a common enemy. And there is a subtle hint that Deputy has been watching the choirmaster on his own account; he is unusually familiar with Jasper's place of residence.

"Lookie yonder," he says to Datchery, who has asked him the way to Mr. Tope's. "You see that there winder and door?"

"That's Tope's?"

"Yer lie; it ain't. That's Jarsper's.—Now look t'other side the harch; not the side where Jarsper's door is; t'other side."

"I see."

"A little way in, o' that side, there's a low door, down two steps. That's Topeseses with 'is name on a hoval plate."

Yes; Deputy is unusually familiar with the choirmaster's abode.

When Datchery and the boy meet for the last time in the final chapter, Deputy has reached such a point of intimacy in his relationship with the white-haired stranger that he calls him "Dick." And Datchery addresses the lad by a new name: "Winks."

"But, I say, don't yer go a-making my name public. I never means to plead to no name, mind yer. When they says to me in the Lockup, a-going to put me down in the book, 'What's your name?' I says to them, 'Find out.' Likewise when they says, 'What's your religion?' I says, 'Find out.' "

From which I conclude that Datchery has told his young agent that he is watching Jasper; that he means to bring him to justice; and that Deputy may one day have to give testimony in court.

We learn at a later stage of this conversation that Deputy is on familiar terms with the Opium Woman. His knowledge of her addiction to the drug—he speaks of her as " 'Er Royal Highness the Princess Puffer"—and of the fact that she lives in London among the "Jacks; and Chayner men; and hother Knifers," confirms my belief that the old crone spent some time at the Travellers' Twopenny before she met Edwin Drood on the day before Christmas.

We discover that Deputy is to ascertain the Opium Woman's exact address; this errand gives us concrete proof that Datchery intends to use the boy as his agent.

Some commentators believe that Deputy is related to one of the major characters in the story; that he is the illegitimate son of John Jasper; or that he is some kin to the Opium Woman. Such assumptions are undoubtedly based on the fact that Dickens had often introduced relationships of this sort in previous novels—Smike's, for example. I find no justification for such belief in the text as we have it, and I am content to consider Deputy an agent of Dick Datchery's; an instrument to be used in bringing John Jasper to trial for murder.

I find it necessary to say a few words about Bazzard, the angular clerk of old Hiram Grewgious, and his tragedy "The Thorn of Anxiety," which no one wished to bring out. I shall not recapitulate here the arguments presented in an earlier study to prove that he cannot possibly be associated with the Datchery assumption. I would simply direct the reader's attention to chapter xx of the novel, wherein Rosa flees to her guardian in London, and wherein old Grewgious dwells at such length on the play written by his clerk. It is hard to conceive of Dickens devoting so much space to "The Thorn of Anxiety" if it were to have no further bearing on his story. What was to be its ultimate purpose must forever remain one of the book's minor mysteries. When Dickens writes, "It was not hard to divine that Mr. Grewgious had related the Bazzard history thus freely, at least quite as much for the recreation of his ward's mind from the subject that had driven her there, as for the gratification of his own tendency to be social and communicative," I am sure he does so with his tongue in his cheek. There is clearly something more than meets the eye in the old lawyer's long-winded account of the tragedy, and I feel certain that Dickens meant to develop this particular aspect of his plot to a greater extent. Just how he would have done so is beyond any logical suggestion I can offer. But there was in Cloisterham a "drooping and despondent little theatre," and in the unwritten part of the novel it may have been destined to become famous as the shrine wherein "The Thorn of Anxiety" came out at last. Since the author of the tragedy was "a gloomy person," I somehow associate that attributive adjective with those qualifying the little theater.

Mr. Luke Honeythunder, that bumptious philanthropist with the

voice of Stentor, seems a very minor personage indeed to have any
influence on the mystery or the eventual ramifications of the plot.
And yet when Minor Canon Crisparkle visits him in the London
chief offices of the Haven of Philanthropy six months after the disappearance of Edwin Drood, Mr. Honeythunder makes a statement that calls for some consideration. He has turned over to the
Minor Canon the accounts of his late wards, Neville and Helena
Landless, now of age, for Mr. Crisparkle has undertaken to accept
them. And he has expressed his opinion that Mr. Crisparkle should
have enrolled himself as a member of the Society. Then he adds:
"I might think one of your profession better employed in devoting
himself to the discovery and punishment of guilt than in leaving
that duty to be undertaken by a layman."

What is the full implication of this remark, revealing as it does
the fact that Mr. Honeythunder is aware of John Jasper's relentless
pursuit of his late ward, Neville Landless? Who, in Cloisterham,
has informed Honeythunder of the choirmaster's efforts? Has John
Jasper himself been in contact with the philanthropist? I have no
answers to these questions, but they inevitably raise themselves in
my mind whenever I reread the passage. Was Honeythunder eventually to join with Sapsea, and thus make a team of jackasses? We
do know that the statement I have quoted is in a part of the chapter
excised by Dickens himself when he read the proof. John Forster
saw the last three numbers of the story through publication; in his
capacity of literary executor to the novelist, he allowed the excision
to remain, along with several others. Perhaps I am making a moun-
tain out of a molehill; certainly we shall never know whether
Forster had sufficient knowledge of the subsequent plot development to justify him in his decision to include this material stricken
out by Dickens. Here again I am inclined to believe that we are
faced with a minor mystery, but one of no great importance. It is a
foregone conclusion, however, that Luke Honeythunder would
have received a sound moral thrashing from the hands of his creator
before the novel was over, had Dickens lived to complete it. To

deduce more than that would be to delve into the mine of pure speculation.

There is no question in my mind, however, that mesmerism, animal magnetism, or hypnotism as we know it today, was to play a highly important part in the second half of *Edwin Drood*. It is my belief that hypnotism alone explains John Forster's statement concerning the novel, "the originality of which was to consist in the review of the murderer's career by himself at the close, when its temptations were to be dwelt upon as if, *not he the culprit, but some other man,* were the tempted." (The italics are mine.) It was inevitable, I contend, that Dickens would one day use hypnotism as a major element in one of his novels, for he was himself an able mesmerist.

As early as 1842 he had written to John Forster: "And speaking of magnetism, let me tell you that the other night at Pittsburgh, there being present only Mr. Q. and the portrait-painter, Kate sat down, laughing, for me to try my hand upon her. I had been holding forth upon the subject rather luminously, and asserting that I thought I could exercise the influence, but had never tried. In six minutes, I magnetized her into hysterics, and then into the magnetic sleep. I tried again next night, and she fell into the slumber in a little more than two minutes—I can wake her with perfect ease; but I confess (not being prepared for anything so sudden and complete) I was on the first occasion rather alarmed."

Again, in 1849, Dickens wrote to his friend Forster: "Ever since I wrote to you Leech has been seriously worse, and again very heavily bled. The night before last he was in such an alarming state of restlessness, which nothing could relieve, that I proposed to Mrs. Leech to try magnetism. Accordingly, in the middle of the night I fell to; and after a very fatiguing bout of it, put him to sleep for an hour and thirty-five minutes. A change came on in the sleep, and he is decidedly better. I talked to the astounded little Mrs. Leech across him, when he was asleep, as if he had been a truss of hay.— What do you think of my setting up in the magnetic-line with a large brass plate? 'Terms, twenty-five guineas per nap.' "

Mamie Dickens supplies a bit of evidence concerning the dynamic power possessed by her father. Writing in a more serious vein, she states in *My Father as I Recall Him:* "I can remember now, as if it were yesterday, how the touch of his hand—he had a most sympathetic touch—was almost too much sometimes, the help and hope in it making my heart full to overflowing. He believed firmly in the power of mesmerism, as a remedy in some forms of illness, and was himself a mesmerist of no mean order; I know of many cases, my own among the number, in which he used his power in this way with perfect success."

Additional evidence is afforded by Gladys Storey, who writes in *Dickens and Daughter:* "Subsequent to the birth of Mrs. Perugini [Kate Dickens] her father became acquainted with Doctor John Elliotson, the physician (the first doctor to use the stethoscope), who practised mesmerism upon those of his patients who expressed a preference to this method of treatment for their ailments. He founded a mesmeric hospital, and Thackeray dedicated *Pendennis* to him out of gratitude for his services.

"Dickens became deeply interested in the subject, and it was not long before he tried to produce the mesmeric coma upon his wife, when he discovered that he possessed quite remarkable powers of animal magnetism.—Mrs. Perugini recollected her father trying to alleviate her in this way during an illness, but they were too temperamentally alike for it to take effect. Yet with her sister, Mamie, his powers were entirely successful."

Concerning Dr. John Elliotson, mentioned above, Robert W. Marks, author of *The Story of Hypnotism,* has the following interesting information: "... his contribution to the scientific extension of hypnotism was enormous. Although he had no insight into its essential nature, he was far ahead of his contemporaries in sensing its therapeutic importance. His experiments convinced him that mesmerism had far-reaching value in the treatment of those disorders we now classify as *psychoneuroses,* that it was a useful prescription in many medical cases, and that it was able to offset the torture and terrors of the then pre-chloroform surgery."

That Charles Dickens had done some reading on the subject is inferable from an article written by Dame Una Pope-Hennessy, author of one of the most recent lives of the novelist. I quote from this article, which appeared in *The Dickensian* for 1945 with the title "The Gad's Hill Library." "His clergyman friend, Chauncey Hare Townshend, who was one of the first Englishmen to study Animal Magnetism abroad, presented him with a copy of his book, 'Mesmerism,' and next to it on a shelf stood another friend's book, 'Human Physiology,' in which Dr. Elliotson described surgical operations carried out on patients in a state of hypnotic trance."

I consider of the greatest significance, however, in its bearing on *Edwin Drood,* the ensuing letter written by Charles Dickens to Sheridan Le Fanu after the novelist had actually begun work on his final manuscript:

> Gad's Hill Place, Higham by Rochester, Kent
> Wednesday Twenty-Fourth November, 1869

My Dear Sir,—In reply to your obliging letter, I beg to assure you that I shall be truly glad to count upon you as a very frequent contributor.

Your sketch is very new, striking, and touching. It should make a remarkable story.

Let me explain to you that I am now about to begin to publish in All the Year Round (at the end of each No.) a serial story by Fitzgerald, of about one good volume in length. A longer serial story being always in course of publication at the same time, and each No. containing only 24 pages, it is desirable that the rest of the matter should be always at such times, if possible, complete in itself. For the reason that the public have a natural tendency, having more than two serial stories to bear in mind at once, to jumble them all together, and do justice to none of them.

I think the enclosed letter will interest you, as showing how very admirably the story of Green Tea[1] was told. It is from the lady I mentioned to you in a note, who has, for thirty or forty years been the subject of far more horrible spectral illusions than have ever, within my knowledge, been placed on record.

She is an English lady, married to a foreigner of good position, and long resident in an old Italian city—its name you will see on the letter—Genoa. I became an intimate friend of her husband's when I was living in Genoa five and twenty years ago, and, seeing that she suffered most frightfully from tic (I knew of her having no other disorder, at the time), I confided to her husband

---

[1] "Green Tea," by Sheridan Le Fanu; in *All the Year Round,* October–November, 1869.

that I had found myself to possess some rather exceptional power of animal magnetism (of which I had tested the efficacy in nervous disorders), and that I would gladly try her. She never developed any of the ordinarily-related phenomena, but after a month began to sleep at night—which she had not done for years, and to change, amazingly to her own mother, in appearance. She then disclosed to me that she was, and had long been, pursued by myriads of bloody phantoms of the most frightful aspect, and that, after becoming paler, they had all *veiled their faces*. From that time, wheresoever I travelled in Italy, she and her husband travelled with me, and every day I magnetized her, sometimes under olive trees, sometimes in vineyards, sometimes in the travelling carriage, sometimes at wayside inns during the mid-day halt. Her husband called me up to her, one night at Rome, when she was rolled into an apparently impossible ball, by tic in the brain, and I only knew where her head was by following her long hair to its source. Such a fit had always held her before at least 30 hours, and it was so alarming to see that I had hardly any belief in myself with reference to it. But in half an hour she was peacefully and naturally asleep, and next morning was quite well.

When I left Italy that time, the spectres had departed. They returned by degrees as time went on, and have ever since been as bad as ever. She has tried other magnetism, however, and has derived partial relief. When I went back to Genoa for a few days, a dozen years ago, I asked her should I magnetize her again? She replied that she *felt* the relief would be immediate; but that the agony of leaving it off so soon, would be so great, that she would rather suffer on.

She is, as you will see, a very brave woman, and has thoroughly considered her disorder. But her sufferings are unspeakable; and if you could write me a few lines giving her any such knowledge as she wants, you would do an action of equally unspeakable kindness.—My Dear Sir,—Faithfully yours always.

Why, in the course of a business letter dealing to some extent with the problems of editorial policy in regard to magazine publication, should Dickens have recounted—with so vivid a wealth of detail—his quarter-of-a-century-old Italian adventure in mesmerism? Undoubtedly his account was partly due to the letter he had received from the English lady. She was the wife of Mr. De la Rue, a Swiss banker, and Dickens had found her to be an "affectionate, excellent little" woman. But I contend that the fullness of his narrative to Le Fanu was in a larger measure occasioned by the fact that once again animal magnetism *per se* was occupying his mind, and that it was doing so because he intended to feature it in *Edwin*

Drood. My contention seems to be justified when certain scenes of the novel are subjected to a critical analysis along mesmeric lines.[2]

There are at least six distinct places in *Edwin Drood* where we may observe the power of animal magnetism in operation. The first reference to the phenomenon occurs in the third chapter, when Dickens writes: "As, in some cases of drunkenness, and in others of animal magnetism, there are two states of consciousness which never clash, but each of which pursues its separate course as though it were continuous instead of broken (thus, if I hide my watch when I am drunk, I must be drunk again before I can remember where), so Miss Twinkleton has two distinct and separate phases of being." We have here, of course, more than a faint echo of the famous episode in Wilkie Collins's *The Moonstone* wherein Franklin Blake, under the influence of laudanum, reënacts his removal of the yellow diamond by going through the same series of actions which he performed on the original occasion of his purloining it when he was under the effects of the same drug. Perhaps Dickens made with deliberate intent this none too indirect allusion to the highly popular tale he was out to surpass; certainly he was not suggesting that John Jasper would destroy his nephew in an opium-induced dream and later confess to a murder which had been successfully accomplished only within his mind. If such were the case, Edwin Drood would not have disappeared. Nor did Jasper attempt to murder his nephew while under the effects of the drug, fail in the undertaking, but actually think he had been successful. We have seen that he did not indulge in opium prior to the murder.

---

[2] Derived from the name of its great exponent, Franz Anton Mesmer, mesmerism, or animal magnetism, involved the idea that a sort of current flowed from one endowed with peculiar powers into the persons or inanimate objects touched by his hands. At first Mesmer believed that magnets were capable of transferring the universal fluid of the atmosphere into the bodies of his patients; he also believed that the fluid was possessed of healing properties. When he discovered that he could produce the same effects upon his patients by using articles devoid of any magnetic quality, he changed his conception of the phenomenon. He decided that it was the power within the practitioner as such that produced the results obtained; this power he called "animal magnetism." Today we should probably say with Bernheim, often called the father of modern hypnotism, that hypnotism "is merely a state of acute susceptibility to suggestion." See Robert W. Marks, *The Story of Hypnotism*, p. 24.

And if Dickens's manuscript "Plans" prove anything at all, they prove that the choirmaster was acting throughout in accordance with a definite, carefully considered scheme for murder. Nor was John Jasper a dual personality in the psychological sense, although there went on within him—as in all men—the ever-present struggle between good and evil. That passage about animal magnetism has thrown many a commentator off the track; I see in it little more than Dickens's own peculiar way of informing his readers that the phenomenon was to be a feature of the novel.

We see animal magnetism at work for the first time when Rosa and Edwin are seated outside the cathedral windows after their lovers' quarrel described at length in this same third chapter. They listen to the organ and the choir.

"I fancy I can distinguish Jack's voice," Edwin remarks.

" 'Take me back at once, please,' urges his Affianced, quickly laying her light hand upon his wrist. 'They will all be coming out directly; let us get away. O, *what a resounding chord!* But don't let us stop to listen to it; let us get away!' " (The italics are mine.)

John Jasper here projects himself through the dominant chord of organ music, and Rosa receives the full impact of his personality and passion for her in the vibrant tones.

This episode is but a prelude to the more striking piano scene in the seventh chapter. Mr. Crisparkle and his mother are gathered with their guests in the drawing room after the dinner given in honor of Helena and Neville Landless. Jasper, seated at the piano, accompanies Rosa while she sings. And Dickens tells us that "he followed her lips most attentively, with his eyes as well as hands; carefully and softly hinting the key-note from time to time." Here, just as before, is the mesmerist in action, forcing himself and his unwelcome love upon the singer through the insistent note. And the choirmaster mesmerizes his pupil into a state bordering on hysteria, for she finally bursts into tears and shrieks out: "I can't bear this! I am frightened! Take me away!"

It is on this occasion that Dickens makes us aware that Helena Landless is to be Rosa's champion; that she, too, is possessed of the mesmeric gift. When Edwin, with his usual obtuseness, remarks: "Pussy's not used to an audience; that's the fact. She got nervous, and couldn't hold out. Besides, Jack, you are such a conscientious master, and require so much, that I believe you make her afraid of you. No wonder," Helena repeats: "No wonder." She has recognized to a far greater degree than Edwin the mechanism of mesmerism.

And when Edwin exclaims: "There, Jack, you hear! You would be afraid of him, under similar circumstances, wouldn't you, Miss Landless?" she answers: "Not under any circumstances."

Surely Dickens has informed us that circumstances of such moment will eventually arise that Helena will confront Jasper in a contest involving their respective mesmeric powers.

Later in the same chapter, when the two young women are in the bedroom they are to share in the Nuns' House and Rosa is pouring her heart out to Helena, the harassed girl says of Jasper to her new-found friend: "He haunts my thoughts, like a dreadful ghost. I feel that I am never safe from him. I feel as if he could pass in through the wall when he is spoken of."

Again John Jasper projects himself through his peculiar power, for the mesmeric force was believed to be capable of penetrating and passing through any obstacle.

Having clearly established the fact that animal magnetism is to play a major part in the novel, Dickens now abandons it for a while, for he does not care to insist too much upon it. It does not reappear until Minor Canon Crisparkle walks to Cloisterham Weir after the momentous interview with John Jasper and Hiram Grewgious, following Edwin Drood's disappearance. So preoccupied is the good gentleman on this occasion that he does not realize he has reached one of his favorite spots until the sound of falling water makes him aware of his surroundings.

" 'How did I come here!' was his first thought, as he stopped.

" 'Why did I come here!' was his second.

"Then, he stood intently listening to the water. A familiar passage in his reading, about airy tongues that syllable men's names, rose so unbidden to his ear, that he put it from him with his hand, as if it were tangible."

He came to the weir in response to the insistent command of John Jasper, who willed him to go there through his mesmeric power; he came to the weir because the choirmaster wanted him to find Edwin's watch and chain and his shirt pin, planted there in the night by the choirmaster. And the reference to Milton's *Comus,* wherein is found the line, "And airy tongues that syllable men's names," enables Dickens to suggest that Minor Canon Crisparkle is aware that Jasper sent him—so much aware, indeed, that he makes a motion with his hand as though to repel the man himself.

But he came to the weir before Edwin's jewelry had been planted; his microscopic eyesight, his minute examination of the posts and timbers, and three separate and distinct references to the starlight making all things visible prove that fact. And so "the Weir ran through his broken sleep all night," until in the morning he revisits the place and finds what Jasper meant him to find.

The final use of animal magnetism in the fragment is made when Jasper pours out his unholy passion for Rosa by the sun dial in the garden of the Nuns' House. The choirmaster exercises his strange power throughout the episode, as will be readily seen from the following quotations:

1. "The moment she sees him from the porch, leaning on the sun-dial, the old horrible feeling of being compelled by him, asserts its hold upon her. She feels that she would even then go back, but that he draws her feet towards him." Note the use of the verb form "draws," as with a magnet.

2. "He would begin by touching her hand. She feels the intention [she is not looking at him, it should be remembered], and draws her hand back. His eyes are then fixed upon her, she knows, though her own see nothing but the grass."

3. "After several times forming her lips, which she knows he is closely watching..."

4. "She is conscious of his looking at her with a gloating admiration..."

5. "Again Rosa quails before his threatening face, though innocent of its meaning, and she remains."

6. "The frightful vehemence of the man, now reaching its full height, so additionally terrifies her as to break the spell that has held her to the spot."

7. "Rosa faints in going up-stairs, and is carefully carried to her room and laid down on her bed."

Here we have seen Jasper the mesmerist at his work of so dominating the girl he madly loves that she faints, through a sort of defense mechanism, in order to blot out the horror she has endured. Yet at the very opening of the following chapter Dickens says: "Rosa no sooner came to herself than the whole of the late interview was before her. It even seemed as if it had pursued her into her insensibility, and she had not had a moment's unconsciousness of it."

I cannot conceive of Dickens cutting the element of animal magnetism from his novel after so many evidences of its function in the half he had completed. And I firmly believe that Jasper was to be hypnotized before he would tell how he had murdered Edwin. Since Helena Landless is the only character in the story capable of outsmarting Jasper at his own mesmeric game, it seems to me inevitable that she will be the one to bring about his confession. When we consider that she is the twin sister of Neville; that the two are "much alike; both very dark, and very rich in colour"; that she had on four occasions "dressed as a boy," and shown "the daring of a man," we may be certain that she was to confront Jasper in the guise of her brother. She was to have done so, I believe, after Jasper was finally captured, and after he had in some way brought about Neville's death. Then and then only, as I see it, would Helena have been able to dominate the mind of the choirmaster, who was himself a mesmerist of no mean ability. Picture Jasper in the condemned cell, convicted of the murders of Edwin Drood and Neville Landless. Suddenly, and at night, Helena appears before him, dressed in her brother's clothes. Would that not be a situation to stir the imagination of Dickens, to quicken his pen, to justify his statement to John Forster that he had "a very curious and new idea for" his "new story"? And how true it would be when the novelist went on to say: "Not a communicable idea (or the interest of the book would be gone), but a very strong one, though difficult to work." Under such circumstances as I have outlined, John Forster had every reason to write, as he did, that "the originality" of *Edwin Drood* "was to consist in the review of the murderer's career by himself at the close, when its temptations were to be dwelt upon as if, not he the culprit, but some other man, were the tempted. The last chapters were to be written in the condemned cell, to which his wickedness, *all elaborately elicited from him as if told of another,* had brought him." (The italics are mine.)

And so we were to have Jasper's confession, written by himself as of another man, for he will have ceased to be the choirmaster known to Cloisterham and will have become a terror-stricken wretch facing the gallows; and this confession will have been "elicited from him as if told of another" through the mechanism of mesmerism, when he will not be conscious of his own identity.

Thus do I read the stars.

Having exhausted the landmarks, both great and small, that might with justification be considered to afford clues to the unwritten half of the novel, I have only to record my own ideas concerning the development it might have had if Charles Dickens had lived to complete it. It is of course impossible to determine in what order Dickens would have handled this or that angle of the plot, or to what degree he would have further emphasized all or several of the characters already introduced. I do feel certain, however, that he would have added no other persons of any great importance. Whether or not I have read the stars with any degree of accuracy, I am convinced that what I have to say in my closing paragraphs would enter into the second half of *Edwin Drood.*

Dick Datchery would capitalize on the fact that the Opium Woman was eager to blackmail Jasper, merely to obtain money from him. He would eventually learn from her all that she knew or suspected, and would acquire valuable information from both Durdles and Deputy. There might even be a repetition of the "un-

accountable expedition," as Professor Jackson has suggested, with
Datchery accompanying the old stonemason in lieu of Jasper.
Datchery would ultimately instruct the Princess Puffer to inform
Jasper about the ring of diamonds and rubies carried by Edwin
Drood upon his person the night he was murdered. The choirmaster would then make a nocturnal visit to the Sapsea tomb—the
secret burial place of his nephew—to obtain the ring, not only because it was a damning piece of evidence against him, but because
he would see in it the "missing link" destined to prove the undoing
of Neville Landless. John Jasper would be met at the tomb by
Datchery, Tartar, Minor Canon Crisparkle, and young Landless.
The ring would be taken from him, and would establish beyond
a reasonable doubt not only the identity of his murdered nephew
but also the exact place of his burial. As I have argued in a previous
study, Dickens was proceeding on the erroneous assumption that
quicklime completely destroys a cadaver, whereas the scientific
truth of the matter reveals the fact that it acts as a preservative.

In a desperate effort to escape, Jasper would break away from
his captors and climb to the summit of the cathedral tower, with the
intention of committing suicide. He would, however, be taken by
Tartar and Crisparkle before he accomplished his purpose; but he
would again break away from them long enough to attack Neville
Landless and throw him from the tower. Entrance to the stairway
being cut off, Jasper might try to climb down the outside of the
tower. But Tartar and Crisparkle would be after him, and force
him back to safety. I have considered such a possibility only because
the climbing abilities of both men have been stressed in the first half
of the novel. And I have often wondered whether Dickens had read
Notre Dame de Paris, by Victor Hugo, whom he admired, and if
so, whether the tragic end of Dom Claude Frollo might not have
suggested some similar treatment centering about the cathedral
tower in *Edwin Drood*. I am sure, at any rate, that Neville would
not have died before learning that his name had been cleared of
all suspicion.

Jasper would be charged with the murders of Edwin Drood and Neville Landless, and after his trial, not to be a major feature of the novel, he would be placed in the condemned cell. As I have already contended, he would be confronted there by Helena Landless in the guise of her brother, and there she would force him by means of her mesmeric power to confess the details of Edwin's murder. He would be hanged by the neck until dead, and would thus make good his oath: "That I will fasten the crime of the murder of my dear dead boy upon the murderer. And, That I devote myself to his destruction."

Sapsea and Honeythunder would surely be confounded. We should, I believe, learn more about Bazzard, whose tragedy "The Thorn of Anxiety" would be produced at last. And we should have more of the delightful skirmishing between Miss Twinkleton and the Billickin. Rosa would marry Lieutenant Tartar, but it would be Hiram Grewgious who, for the sake of sentiment, would place the ring of diamonds and rubies upon her finger. Minor Canon Crisparkle would marry Helena Landless.

Such is my brief summary of what might have been; but how cold and feeble it sounds when I think of the warmth and dramatic power that would have quickened it if Charles Dickens had only lived! But his creative genius would function no more after that 8th of June, 1870, and *The Mystery of Edwin Drood* will forever remain a half-told tale. Being a tale told by a master writer, it is full of pregnant possibilities, signifying something. What does it mean to the reader of today? Mr. V. S. Pritchett, in *The Living Novel,* gives a forceful answer to the question: *"Edwin Drood* stands at the parting of the ways between the early Victorian and the modern attitude to murder in literature, and also, I suspect, at the beginnings of a change in Dickens himself. The earlier murders of Dickens belong to the more turbulent decades of the nineteenth century. By the late 'fifties a calm had been reached; the lid had been levered back on to the pot of society and its seething had become a prosperous simmer. When Wilkie Collins wrote *The Moonstone* and Dickens, not to be outdone, followed it with *Edwin Drood,* we begin the long career of murder for murder's sake, murder which illustrates nothing and is there only to stimulate our skill in detection and to distract us with mystery. The sense of guilt is so transformed that we do not seek to expiate it vicariously on the stage; we turn upon the murderer and hunt him down. Presently, in our time, the hunt degenerates into the conundrums of the detective novel which, by a supreme irony, distracts us from our part in the mass murders of two wars. One or two critics have suggested that the struggle with the unfamiliar technique of the hunt was too much for Dickens and that it killed him and his novel. We cannot know whether this is so; but both those who dismiss the book as the last leaden effort of a worn-out man, and those who observe that it is the most careful and private of Dickens's novels, are agreed that it is pitched in a key he has never struck before."

It is indeed so pitched, for its central theme is the enigma of a man's soul torn by the eternal struggle between good and evil—a soul whose internal warfare is rendered the more dramatic because it belongs not only to John Jasper, choirmaster and murderer, but also to Charles Dickens, a great literary artist. And when Mr. Pritchett closes his penetrating essay on the novel by saying that "the kind of realism employed in *Edwin Drood* reads like an attempt to reconstruct and co-ordinate his [Dickens's] world, like a preparation for a final confession of guilt," I believe he has come close to the heart of the matter. As always, in this fragment destined to remain forever a great mystery, Charles Dickens had something to say to us. I have already suggested that in his *alter ego* John Jasper he was taking himself to task for having sinned against the moral code of his day and the deeper, finer instincts of his nature.

The Mystery of Edwin Drood has been and is now—for me, at least—a fascinating subject for speculation. It is my hope that the studies I have written may stimulate further interest in the novel and its author, and that other appraisals or solutions may be forthcoming. Beginning as "an amiable hobby that shies at nothing and kicks nobody," my effort to unravel the mystery has become an engrossing avocation—a real labor of love. I do not feel that this labor has come to an end because I have completed the five studies I had planned or because I have done with what might have been. In that fragmentary firmament which Charles Dickens called *The Mystery of Edwin Drood* the stars shine on, and I may still fix my gaze upon them, seeking for the letters I have yet to learn.